# worship:

# wedding to marriage

German **martinez**

D0066965

The Pastoral Press

Washington, DC

ISBN: 1-56929-009-1

The Pastoral Press
225 Sheridan Street, N.W.
Washington, D.C. 20011
(202) 723-1254

The Pastoral Press is the publications division of the National Association of Pastoral Musicians, a membership organization of musicians and clergy dedicated to fostering the art of musical liturgy.

Printed in the United States of America

*To Jesús Arias (+ 1993) and María Martínez*

*and my niece and nephews*

# Contents

# Introduction

THE INSTITUTION OF MARRIAGE HAS BEEN SUBJECT TO MANY SIGNIFI-
cant influences in this last half of the twentieth century. As a
consequence it has been much studied by the social sciences
and is a subject of much commentary by the pundits of popular culture. Whereas studies on the psychodynamics and social phenomena superabound, not enough has been written
on the central reality of the mystery of marriage. This core reality has remained for the most part unattended in secular literature. Also, until a few decades ago Western Christian
Churches have focused on the legal aspects of marriage. The
progress made by the human sciences in responding to new
social phenomena demands at least a comparable effort on the
part of the church in regard to both the theory and practice of
marriage.

A credible and contemporary theological and spiritual perspective on marriage has to incorporate the insights of the behavioral sciences as well as to understand the complex human
experience that is the real-life context in which marriage is actually experienced. The significant gap existing in this regard
in the past is already being filled by the excellent contributions
of the human sciences which focus on new and integrating
concepts of the person.

The study of the specifically Christian meaning of marriage
must be related to the whole of the salvific story since marriage
is already salvific at its core. Furthermore, the foundational

source of the Christian inspiration and symbolism of marriage, namely, biblical revelation, begins (Gn 2:23-24) and ends (Rv 22:17) with an effusion of marital communion and love.

The insufficiency of theological reflection in approaching the deeper understanding of the central reality of the sacrament has also been acknowledged by the Catholic hierarchy. Cardinal Edouard Gagnon, President of the Pontifical Council for the Family, says:

> But why has there been such a lack of emphasis on the sacrament in modern writing in English on Christian marriage? . . . Did we perhaps tend to avoid looking closely at the sacrament because it is too much of a challenge to us?" . . . Therefore there is a great need today for study which sets forth "sacramentality" in both its specific and wider meanings . . ."[1]

The wide range of critical issues raised today show that the complexity, and even elusive truth, of the marriage reality cannot be reduced to a single formula woven of lofty ideals. Marriage must have a central position in contemporary theological reflection; even more, it must be rooted in a spirituality of the economy of salvation. This is an essential key in approaching many of the problems facing marriage today, including divorce, and in a broader sense in understanding the "sacramentality" which is at the heart of Christian living and, indeed, of life itself.

Marriage as sacrament has always been affirmed in the Catholic Church. Thus the problem does not arise from a lack of theological discussion of the subject, but rather from the lack of a credible presentation of the inner meaning and the all-embracing view of the sacramental experience of human marriage. As a consequence, "the Catholic church has never had a clear and well-developed spirituality for married people, despite her long tradition of seeing matrimony as a sacrament and thus a way of holiness."[2]

Marriage is experienced as a sacrament of life, and thus a way of holiness, when it is seen within the central and larger perspective of worship which celebrates Christ living in the experience of the spouses. The interpretation of the sources of faith—Scripture and tradition—though necessary, can become abstract speculation when they are separated from the experience of worship in which those sources are related to the present human experience and become a living reality. It is this larger sacramentalized experience which provides, not a complete program of married life, but the foundation for a conjugal spirituality.

This leads to the fundamental perspective and unifying theme of this book: Christian worship. What follows explores the reality of the mystery of human experience and the divine action in marriage. Consequently, these chapters examine some of the major themes that are relevant to today's theological reflection and pastoral praxis. The action of worship in itself with its multifold meanings, as well as the concrete marriage ritual, provide the central theological perspective for a revitalized theology of marriage. I do not know of any book that follows this approach.

In fact, both the liturgical action in general and specifically the marriage ritual celebration, which express the various gifts and needs of married persons, are inseparable in understanding the vocation of marriage. The marriage liturgy celebrates the actualized economy of salvation mirrored in the life experience of married Christians and their families and thus provides the basic setting and the symbolic interpretation for understanding the sacramental reality. This sacramental reality becomes in turn the heart of the liturgical experience and of marriage spirituality itself.

Nevertheless, the understanding of any sacrament requires more than the celebrative experience. The critical mediation of theological reflection is also necessary because there is no true celebration without an authentic faith vision. In the particular case of marriage, the insight and the application of a modern anthropological content and biblical theology, together with other elements of the one complex reality of the celebration, are essential. This is, in fact, the rationale behind the two reforms of the marriage rite issued by Rome in 1969 and 1990 respectively.

As indicated, this book focuses on major components of the theological and liturgical perspectives on marriage. The overall content is sequential and has been woven together to provide a consistent thematic development in three parts: Experience, Tradition, and Celebration.

Part I presents the experience of marriage from the perspective of the mystery of worship as such and from the personalist understanding of the whole of the marital and intimate life which forms a community of persons.

Marriage and worship are two universal realities. Although both are historical, they transcend the realities in which they are rooted. The analogy between worship and marriage is relevant to the articulation of the core of the theology of marriage. From this very core a foundation to conjugal spirituality emerges regarding four essential areas: agape-love, mutual self-giving, communication, and faith sharing.

For its part, "Marriage as Communion" demonstrates that the neglect of the human values of marriage or, more precisely, the lack of a personalist anthropology and an adequate theological consideration of sexuality have been at the root of the weakness of the traditional approach to marriage. Marriage through the symbolic model of the communion of love, presented as a living sign of salvation by *Gaudium et Spes*, has resulted in a paradigmatic shift in the contemporary Christian vision of marriage.

Part II explores the Christian tradition from two complementary perspectives: first, the development of the ritual from secular to ecclesiastical marriage; second, the theological tradition and the meaning of marriage sacramentality. In each of these two perspectives the patristic and medieval churches maintained their pastoral concerns and a particular vision of marriage sacramentality.

The Eastern Churches not only inculturated the pre-Christian Greco-Roman rituals, but also expressed a rich theology and spirituality in the passage and vocation of marriage in their rites. The Western Churches also inculturated local customs, but did not develop a liturgical theology of marriage. The complex history of the development of marriage rite and historical theology helps us to understand the breath of the different Christian traditions, and thus come closer to the meaning of "Tradition" in the fullest sense of the word. This is essential in order to develop new pastoral approaches to the crises facing marriage today.

Part III focuses on initiation, ritualization, and doctrine. The three parts of this triptych study marriage as follows: first, within the dynamics of the initiatory process from the anthropological, pastoral, historical and cultural perspectives. Second, its ritual celebration is considered in the context of the mystery of love and the mystery of life. Third, the potential for growth into spiritual maturity is emphasized from the viewpoint of the covenantal vision which the rich biblico-liturgical content of the marriage liturgy provides.

Within this overall consideration of the ritual celebration, two other symbolic models of marriage are stressed: vocation and covenant, which complement and are inseparable from communion and sacrament. The revised Roman marriage rite (1990) is reviewed in chapter six: its doctrinal content, ritual structure, and the liturgical elements of the celebration are presented and analyzed; but the other two chapters also contain explicit references to the new rite and follow its inspirational and doctrinal guidelines.

Although the public wedding ceremony should provide the complete expression of the spiritual and human aspects of a partnership whose essence is love, marriage is preeminently a blessed bond which, like the act of worship itself, is only fully expressed in the totality of life. In responding to the divine activity which permeates all human existence, we realize that the ongoing life of every member of the faithful, and indeed of every marriage, is sacramental, a holy union of the divine and human.

Many individuals have enriched and challenged me with their support and valuable suggestions in the process of writing a number of these chapters which grew out of my pastoral experience, research, and teaching a course on marriage. First, I would like to express special thanks to my students, faculty colleagues, and the Dean, Fr. Vincent Novak, S.J., of the Graduate School of Religion and Religious Education of Fordham University. I am also grateful to William Mc Shea, Professor Emeritus of Carlow College, Pittsburgh, for his timely suggestions to improve the literary style of this text, and to the director of The Pastoral Press, Larry Johnson, for his graciousness and expert guidance in publishing this work.

*Notes*

1. Peter J. Elliot, *What God Has Joined . . . The Sacramentality of Marriage* (New York: Alba House, 1990) vii.
2. Charles A. Gallagher and others, *Embodied in Love: Sacramental Spirituality and Sexual Intimacy* (New York: Crossroad, 1984) 1.

# THE EXPERIENCE

# 1

# Marriage as Worship: A Theological Analogy

MARRIAGE AND WORSHIP ARE BOTH PRIMARY AND UNIVERSAL HU-
man realities where manifold dimensions converge: body and
spirit, earthly elements and symbolic actions, natural phenomena and divine mystery. Though historical by their nature,
and always historically related, they essentially transcend the
realities they embody. The pledge of the old Anglican wedding ritual, "with my body I thee worship," speaks profoundly of this central meaning. Like worship, which etymologically
means "ascribing worth to another being," marriage is the total validation of the other in the devotion and service, celebration and mystery of a relationship.[1]

## SYMBOLIC ACTION, DEPTH OF MEANING, SELF-TRANSCENDENCY

Worship, therefore, can be applied to marriage analogously.
This analogy suggests theological concepts which are most relevant in articulating the core of a much needed conjugal spirituality. Marriage and worship are, in fact, a typical case of coherence, even at the strictly anthropological level, from at least
three major perspectives: symbolic action, depth of meaning,
and self-transcendency.[2]

3

Symbolic actions are the language people use to express the experience of both shared beliefs through worship or the shared love of a marital relationship. The nature, the inner reality, of a marital relationship is to be rooted in love, just as the nature of worship is to be grounded in faith. Without belief worship is meaningless; without love marriage is empty. In both cases there is a symbolic and existential relationship. Worship embodies an inner life, a belief through rituals, since the ritual is the cradle of religious belief. It has the proper language and external gesture of inner realities—as does a marital partnership. Its verbal or bodily. expressions, its quality and reality of intimacy, its celebrations and struggles, in summary, the whole interaction of the self-giving and self-serving relationship of a man and a woman in marriage stems from an inner reality of that love. These are—or are not—embodied in love. Spirituality depends on the truthfulness of that relationship whether in marriage or in worship, and that truthfulness will be apparent in the symbolic and existential language of the relationship.

The depth of meaning is envisioned in the many possible orders of reality to which marriage and worship can refer. This is precisely why symbolic actions and language come into the picture. The ordinary experience of a community of love, or a community of faith, provides the metaphors people use to express their value, and the prophetic revelation describes the covenant of God to God's people. Marriage and worship are, in fact, so complex and rich that they are very difficult to define. We all have experienced love—the primary end of marriage—and we all participate in ritual actions, but we take pains to share with others those kinds of experiences. In this aspect the complexity of love and of religious ritual is very clear. This fact bespeaks their intrinsic link and mutual support in various levels of meaning. "Love," says L. Mitchell, "whether of God or of the girl next door, is all but impossible to express except through outward symbolic action, that is, through ritual acts."[3]

Finally, self-transcendency intrinsically defines worship as it does marriage. Any definition of worship, even from the point of view of many anthropologists, centers around this essential dimension, as expressed in Evelyn Underhill's classical definition, "the response of the creature to the Eternal."[4] Similarly, the total reality of a community of marital life and love cannot be understood without the vertical dimension of that created love, the beyond experienced within the encounter between I and Thou. This intimate encounter by its dynamism is enclosed by, and moves toward the ultimate mystery, God himself. God becomes the basis of the encounter, as Martin Buber's interpersonal principle of the eternal Thou demonstrates.[5] Charles Davis, in his classic study of the nature of religious experience and feeling, reaches the same conclusion from a different perspective. "Human feelings," he says, "by their dynamism, point beyond themselves; they are an expression of self-transcendence."[6] The self-giving marital love, as a symbol of divine love, straining toward God, reveals and celebrates the mystery of God; this is worship. True marriage, like true worship, is rooted primarily therefore in self-transcendent love. They both relate to something in the foundations of human consciousness and point beyond their reality. God is thus made present.

This analogical relationship between marriage and worship, which, as stated above, includes symbolic action, depth of meaning, and self-transcendency, underlies the biblical understanding of marriage. Conjugal spirituality can only be properly understood against this background. It is against this background of an eminently human love that the biblical perspective of God's covenant reveals its full depth of meaning.

## THE COVENANT RELATIONSHIP

God's nuptial relationship with his people in the Old Testament becomes the paradigm of the most intimate human relationship. The human experience of love parallels that relationship of fidelity and becomes the most telling metaphor of Israel's covenant. "Marriage, then, is the grammar that God uses to express his love and faithfulness."[7] Similarly, in the New Testament perspective Christ, the lover and husband of humanity,[8] renews the covenant by his sacrifice and becomes the paradigm of Christian marriage. The nuptial reality between Christ and his church is the actual foundation and source of the Christian spirituality of marriage. The Spirit of

the risen Lord inspires the daily living of the spouses in a personal and faithful self-donation.[9]

Worship, more accurately spiritual worship, exemplifies the
ideals of the covenant and consequently of marriage. Israel is
called to offer a spiritual worship of obedience to the word
and to maintain God's covenant, because this covenant is established after Israel's liberation and passage to faith in Yahweh's love and faithfulness. The "chosen and priestly people"
acknowledge this covenant with a life and service of spiritual
worship.[10] The prophets and the psalmists use this same language of worship and marital relationship to dramatize that
love between Yahweh and Israel.[11]

Christ renews the liturgical conception of the prophets "in
spirit and in truth." He dies to establish a new covenant. Very
often the liturgical symbolism of the New Testament is rooted
in the prophets. The reality of the covenant, definitively con-
cluded in Jesus Christ, is evoked by Paul in Ephesians to establish a parallel between marriage and the union of Christ
with his church. The reference here to baptism and the eucharist in the context of the mystery of Christ's cross exemplifies
once more the spiritual foundation of marriage as spiritual
sacrifice. In fact, Christians are called to be themselves a proclamation of praise of God's love, in the image of Christ, who
offered himself up through the Holy Spirit, as the only fitting
worship to God.[12]

## A BIBLICAL THEOLOGY AND SPIRITUALITY

This application of a biblical-liturgical theology to marriage
fills the writings of the early church which, in turn, inspired
the Roman sacramentaries (fifth to eighth century). The later
Roman ritual of marriage, however, beginning in the eleventh
century makes only sporadic reference to this biblical theology
and spirituality of marriage. In its place a contractual mentality arose.[13] In patristic theology, on the contrary, any aspect of
marriage as a contract is notoriously absent. The spiritual perspective of marriage centers around the idea of the mystery of
marriage seen in the nuptial and sacrificial relationship of
Christ and the church. This relationship constitutes the source
and foundation of the theology of marriage in the tradition of
the Fathers.[14]

The Eastern Churches are a telling example of a profound and compelling theological spirituality of marriage along the biblical lines of the covenantal relationship of spiritual sacrifice. They have focused on the agape-sacrifice spirituality of marriage, which constitutes the mystical and sacramental reality of marriage. Man and woman's partnership of love is represented poetically as an icon of a mystery of praise. They are ministers in their priestly vocation of an offering of life and love to each other.[15]

In his classic research on marriage in the east, Cardinal Raes has shown the foundation of this biblical and liturgical spirituality. The splendid eastern rituals present a balance between a highly positive view of conjugal life—an earthly type of spirituality—and a mystical, liturgical theology. Both horizontal and vertical dimensions are rooted in biblical symbolism. It is against the background of the human reality that the church's nuptial offering by Christ at the wedding banquet of the cross is conceived as the foundation of a conjugal spirituality: "Christ-husband, who had married the holy and faithful church, and had given to her at the cenacle his body and blood . . . raise your right hand and bless husband and wife."[16]

This priestly ministry of Christ has nothing to do with sacred objects. By the same token, marriage as worship goes beyond the boundaries of created sacralization. The "one flesh" is holy from its roots only by the created act of God-agape. In this regard, Catholic theology has long ago acknowledged the impact of desacralization in the New Testament, which sees human values observed from the eschatological reality of Christ. "For his is the peace between us . . . and has broken down the barrier . . . destroying in his own person the hostility caused by the rules and decrees of the law" (Eph 2:14-15).[17]

Worship is, therefore, analogously applied to marriage only under this assumption. In its broad sense it embraces all the secular values, the day-to-day experience and the totality of the challenges of becoming one, if lived as a symbol and reality of the transcendent presence of God-agape. The mystery of life embodied in the mystery of Christ is the background and source of an inclusive spirituality of marriage which demands to be celebrated in the mystery of worship.

This divine dimension of the secular sphere of marriage is neither mythical sacralization, nor mystical idealization. E.

Schillebeeckx rightly states that "faith in Yahweh in effect 'desacralized,' or secularized, marriage—took it out of a purely religious sphere and set it squarely in the human, secular sphere."[18] Since marriage is foremost a secular value, Christian spirituality rejects the false dichotomy between sacred and profane and views the presence of the holy in that secular value. Worship, with its secular character, provides the prism of a larger supernatural context.

Mystical idealization, on the other hand, whether concerned with worship or marriage, devalues the goodness and beauty of the order of creation. True religion is rooted in human experience and feeling which are very important channels in the encountering of the mystery of the Holy. Davis accurately puts the question in this way: "How is it, then, that religion, mystical religion particularly, has—with reason—been seen as the enemy of the body and the affections?"[19] As people establish communication in worship with the absolute through symbols, so the partners are drawn into the inner life of God through the mutuality of their bodily and spiritual selves, the total being.

These misinterpretations are at the bottom of the ruinous cleavage between faith and life, and are the cause of alienation of many people from the church in the vital sphere of marriage. Furthermore, they run counter to a theology which presents marriage as the natural sign and milieu of God's saving and healing love.

The lifelong process of initiation in an intimate communion of marital life should thus be seen within the perspective of worship; a praise of the God-agape. This worship perspective rightly generates a vital spirituality which is essential to a vital marriage, because spirituality is the totality of the personal experiences celebrated as a gift of God and in the intimacy with God which is the very meaning of worship. The spouses, in acknowledging God's intimate presence in each other, accept each other as his permanent gift and perfect each other in their own path of spirituality. This intimacy with God empowers them to a life of holiness, in liturgical terms, to be the "memory" of the Lord.

This theological analogy of worship which sacramentally subsumes all human experiences and from which true spirituality unfolds provides a fundamental orientation and unity of conjugal spirituality. It is not a comprehensive panorama of the complex challenges of marriage and family living, but it integrates four vital realities into a whole: agape-love, donation, communication, and faith sharing.

## AGAPE OF INTIMACY, MEAL, AND EUCHARIST

Agape defines the fundamental quality of love and has been applied to the eucharistic meal of intimate fellowship of early Christianity, celebrated at home. This new analogy of worship, based on the spiritually profound, symbolic, and transcendent concept of agape, offers fruitful insights to understanding the core of marriage spirituality.

In fact, the sharing of self and the sharing of a meal in married life are not strictly utilitarian bodily functions only because of agape. Body and bread sharing in this respect are gift and communion, that is, agape. It is an intimate sharing which possesses a symbolic quality of donation and devotion, of reverence and care. The Christian eucharist, as agape-meal and agape offering of the glorious Christ, builds upon the natural significance of that sharing of a fellowship meal. Consequently, mutual intimacy of body and bread are integral to the daily experience of conjugal spirituality, if lived in the spirit of agape as being "in the Lord" (1 Cor 7:39) and celebrated in the source and center of every Christian spirituality, the eucharist.[20]

A cleavage between faith and life in this most important reality of family life on which human growth and fulfillment depend has borne tragic consequences, especially in a world of great change and challenge. This is so because this cleavage cripples conjugal spirituality in its core: the life-giving and life-uniting reality of agape-love of which God himself is the ultimate reality and source, but which has to be lived in the concrete and the human. On the one hand, this kind of love is an irreplaceable gift of being, understood and accepted in the deepest self in rejection of the collective depersonalization of modern society. On the other hand, this self-bestowal in the spirit of agape is the common source in which the spouses meet the Holy and their spirituality unfolds in the day-to-day experiences of life. The God-agape is present in both the exceptional and the common experiences of the spouses, whether in the case of a family meal, or the involvement of a psychological and sexual intimacy, or the entering into the self-offering of Christ. These are only three privileged moments from which an all-embracing home spirituality can be enriched.[21]

The importance of this line of thought stems from the clarifying nature of agape in regard to the ambiguities of love in our present culture. Serious psychological analysis provides the background for a solid understanding of the complex reality of love in answering the question: What is agape?

Agape means a way of being; it is a creative process; it never fails because it is unconditional, self-giving, and self-sacrificing. This productive activity of loving is not a goddess, says Erich Fromm, because the worshiper of the goddess of love becomes passive and loses his or her power. In fact, no one can *have* love because it only exists in the *act of loving*, as Fromm rightly describes it.[22] The mode of "having," so pervasive in contemporary human relations, can be deadening and suffocating. The crises of intimacy with all its human counterfeits and psychological barriers depends on such an existential structure in human relations.

The presence of God makes possible the experience of transcendence through love. The New Testament presents this transcendence as a dynamic relationship with which a person is empowered by the mystery of the divine love. The biblical God is a God of intimacy and passion. In fact, God is simply love (1 Jn 4:8, 16).

Marriage, especially in the theology of John (Jn 2:1-12) and Paul (Eph 5:25, 32), is a total and all-embracing communion after the image of the nuptial sacrifice of Christ, who gives up his nuptial body.[23] The philosophical and psychological analysis often misses this transcendent perspective, but corroborates the teaching of the Scriptures on the same basic human realities of agape. Thus they are essential characteristics of a spirituality of marriage: unconditional, sacrificial, caring, and self-renewing love. Thus "love never ends" (1 Cor 13) because it tells the other person that he or she will never die.[24]

Stressing the importance of the spiritual nature of agape-love, the reality of eros-love is reaffirmed because that transcendent agape would be meaningless without the sexual desire of eros. The exaggerated fear of "keeping perverse desire within its proper bounds"[25] divorced for centuries, at least in theory, sexual passion, tenderness, and intimacy on the one hand, and marriage spirituality on the other. J. Ratzinger draws, in this respect, a cogent biblical analogy: "As the covenant without creation would be empty, so agape without eros is inhuman."[26] Persons are embodied spirits relating symbolically through the language of their body. Profound personal relations demand real personal intimacy in the integrity of a community of love.

A false dichotomy between spirit and flesh has undermined the truth of creation of male and female in the image of God. Furthermore, it has emasculated human sexuality, the capacity to love and procreate, in its physical and spiritual being and doing. The dialogic structure of sexual intimacy, in fact, complements and broadens the being of man and woman,[27] and at the same time, as a saving mystery in faith, symbolizes and causes union with God. Therefore, marital spirituality and sexual intimacy are not enemies but friends, because the author of life and love is present in their sacramental sexual experience. They are called to holiness in intimacy with the divine love through their celebration of the total commitment in a body, soul, and spirit intercourse—"nakedness without shame."[28]

Intimacy expresses the interpersonal capacity of a total life-sharing, not only through the eros of passion, warmth, and mature sexual encounter, but also through the agape of commitment, acceptance, and self-disclosure. Intimacy cannot be reduced to tactility or even sexuality. It is a way of being and relating in closeness to the other in the life-process of creating a community. What Erik Erikson and other social scientists state concerning the conditions for interpersonal intimacy has to be taken seriously in the theological underpinning of conjugal spirituality.[29] The spirituality of marriage takes into account what human scientists have to say because of the secular nature of marriage. They present the real and fertile ground in which the spouses meet the Holy. These human conditions, like the attitude of reverence and devotion, the ideal of unselfish love and spiritual nakedness, the spontaneity of freedom and authenticity, all become true hallmarks of conjugal spirituality. By the same token, competition and stagnation, angelism and repression are rejected. To live humanly in the authentic faith of the passionate and committed God of the covenant is the highest form of intimacy.

In fact, no one has better captured this shared intimacy of God as a love with a passion for truth and life than the prophets, the Song of Songs, the psalmists, or the Christian wisdom of mystics like Teresa of Avila and John of the Cross.[30] A correlation exists between God's touching us deeply and wholly and the experience of human intimacy. To discover this correlation is to discover the key to marital spirituality.

Existential intimacy is, therefore, absolutely necessary for human life. Paradoxically, many people have lost the capacity to share intimacy because of a highly competitive individualism, and this speaks to us of the need to stress it in reference to family life. It calls for total sexual intimacy in marriage, but touches the larger mutuality of the partners' interaction, especially around the family table.

Meals are especially privileged moments of the intimate presence because of the caring and sharing they entail. Their intimate presence is irreplaceable in a society of high mobility in order for the spouses to remain "in touch" and to keep fondness alive. The agape of sharing a meal, as described before, is an integral part of being together. The "I-Thou" character of sharing strengthens a love commitment. It is like a "natural sacrament"[31] of love and life which supports family communication and points in faith to the agape of the eucharist. The intimacy of a meal, like the intimacy of the body, rejects idolization as much as it rejects utilitarianism. Body and food are gifts from God which have to be cherished and treated with reverence. The eucharist, which celebrates the Lord's Supper, brings about a healing of human ambiguities and a deeper celebration of the agape of committed love.

## DAILY DYING AND RISING

Living and dying is the basic pattern of all life. Christian faith paradoxically reverses this natural pattern into a mystery of death into life through the transsignification of human life by worship. This mystery of dying to death itself, an act of transcendental worship, thus belongs to the core of spirituality. Ideally, this spirituality means a radically new manner of relating to others, based on inner personal freedom and the passion of love.

This applies specifically to marriage because of its interpersonal reality; a dependability and independence, where the other spouse in his or her interior space is never fully known or validated. That new life style cannot exist without the couple's experience of a free oblatory love. Modern society, with its greater mobility and its greater expectations from personal relationships, its competition and rejection of the idea of self-service—among other factors—has created a culture where relationships marked by depth of concern and the devotion of faithfulness are the exceptions.

True love is the sign of true freedom, but true freedom in marriage does not exist without a human response to the intimate longing of the other person, and without the coherence of creative fidelity. "There can be no true freedom without our first having emptied ourselves of self, so that we might open ourselves to the only reality capable of fully satisfying our powers of love and knowledge," says Rene Laturelle.[32] The couple encounters that "only reality" in the infinite God through a relationship "in depth" which is characterized by self-control, dependability, and commitment. In the Christian perspective it is a matter of faith and love, because through these gifts Christians have been called to freedom in dying and rising each day. The gift of self (love) results in a possession of self (freedom) and establishes the most intimate and most challenging of all human relationships.

This relationship of marriage is influenced throughout life by internal and external factors which affect each partner and, at the same time, by the different stages of development throughout the family's lifetime. Couples experience the ebb and flow, the ups and downs, the fervor and dryness of life itself. "Marriage," in the words of Mary G. Durkin, "is not a smooth curve drawn on the chart of life. It is, rather, a series of cycles, of deaths and rebirth, of old endings and new beginnings, of falling in love again."[33] The "happily ever after" mentality of a perpetual ecstasy not only builds up false expectations and leads to disillusionment, it denies the paradoxical reality of the life-giving oblative love and forgiveness, the healing and freeing discipline of self-control, and the redemptive idea of purification necessary for any dynamic and creative love relationship.

In today's society it is more than ever apparent that a marital life span consists of various stages or passages which every couple will experience in the course of their relationship. This developmental reality must be seen as the necessary starting point of any understanding of the process of marital relationship. Through the years of change and growth the two become many different people with different needs and expectations. Can marital unity and fulfillment still be maintained in this being and becoming? Certain social scientists insist that it is possible through a "creative marriage" which nurtures the basic values of caring, empathy, mutual respect, equality, trust, and commitment.[34] These basic values are without a doubt the human thread of a covenantal partnership. The pressure of a career, the challenges of parenthood, the disagreements and tensions of the ever-changing modes of modern living, cannot but affect the aliveness of a relationship. A couple hears the call to holiness in this very web of the unending seasons and changing faces of their marital journey.

A spirituality of stability is needed today. It means a spirituality of "staying in love," which embodies, on the one hand, the courage to be a partnership[35]—the existentially strengthening effect of self-donations—and, on the other hand, in Christian terms, the wisdom of the cross—the nuptial journey of Jesus through the total donation and service. The former provides a healthy and dynamic tension against the senescence of time; the latter is a rock of stability against external and internal fragmentive dependencies.

Any attempt to grow and endure based solely on endless analysis, or even developmental ideas of a relationship is bound to fail because the growth of two people is never an automatic process and is always unpredictable and complex. Besides the realistic expectations and life style of each couple, there is a spiritual element which motivates and makes self-knowledge and self-revelation possible. Only authentic faith is transforming and life-giving—no magical effects or external miracles are needed. Nevertheless, since the paradox of the cross, the hallmark of faith, stresses the idea of self-sacrifice and donation, it shows the futility of human self-fulfillment, which actually leads to failure. Religion is not meant to be a guarantee of success, but an unrelenting call to faithfulness. Both the human, which is transient, and the divine, which has an ultimate value, actualize human plenitude.

Dying and rising in marriage reveal the depth of meaning in a spirituality of donation and service. It is the sharing of the paschal mystery. Husband and wife realize that every act of faithfulness is the actualization of the incompleteness of the paschal mystery in them. They marry each other many times in many different ways, always rising to a deeper life. Their living out, in hope, the ideal in the midst of human weakness always brings about growth because of the presence of the cross in their lives, which is their eucharist. The perspective of worship broadens that meaning again, since both eucharistic worship and marriage are covenant signs and the actualization of God's love.[36]

From the altar of their everyday experience through which they build an irreplaceable community of love and minister to each other in the domestic church, the spouses offer the concrete unfolding of their spiritual sacrifice to God.[37] The specific applications of this realistic spirituality are numerous. The playful, caring, earthly, and meaning-bestowing atmosphere of the house provides the ideal milieu to live authentic worship, but it needs the ritual celebration which can transfigure and heal the fragility of human relations through the force of the celebrated divine life.

## GIFT-GIVEN COMMUNICATION

Communication is the lifeblood of the interpersonal communion of the partners. The quality of their relationship has many different degrees of actualization because it rises and falls as the couple's sharing does. It is either an authentic encounter or the failure of encounter. This interpersonal communion is a great challenge because it reveals, on the one hand, the uniqueness of each individual and appears, on the other hand, as a self-gift, which has to be acknowledged as such by either spouse. Created by an inviolable interiority, which constitutes my freedom and my human dignity, I am gifted with words and love to validate the existence of the other. I surrender freely what I freely received—my very self—in the encounter with another person.

Theological reflection is not yet implied, at this anthropological level of one's need for relating to another. A totally new dimension of the spirituality of the spouses in striving for effective communication in giving and sharing is opened up in light of the mystery of God's self-communication. Analogies that provide a model for a life-generating communication can be drawn from a theology of divine revelation.

Revelation is a happening of God's unconditional love, expressed in mysterious ways, in deeds and words to humankind all throughout history. This happening of God's initiative leads to an encounter with the people, and lets the people know how much God can do for them. In the sharing of the living reality of God's own self, people participate in the eternal truth resulting in the development of their full potential for being. This participation is actualized in the mystery of worship, since worship is revelation and gift-given communication. And so is marriage.

The forms of communication in the historical revelation of Scripture, as in the marital relationship are inexhaustible. The analogies of both cases, however, lead to the same conclusive characteristics of essential communication: dialogue, communion, presence, and power.

Dialogue through empathy and freedom is vital to human relations. The importance of dialogue as a keystone of effective communication stems from the dialogic structure of human existence. In his existential visions of human reality, Buber not only stressed the intersubjectivity of human communication, but saw this interpersonal reality linked intrinsically to God's reality and the way to God. God is mysteriously mirrored in the relationship with the other. This interpersonal and transcendent vision has been blurred in a modern consumeristic society.[38]

If the sacredness of personhood is the basis of any meaningful dialogue, the well-being of the other is the goal of marital dialogue. Quality dialogue, based on sincere devotion to human dignity and radical acceptance of mutuality, leads to effective communication. Couples who develop the right attitudes of creative communication (which is an art, not an information technique), speak in open and honest language, conveying ideas and emotions, listening and sharing, affirming and encouraging.

These are the central aspects of loving-giving communication. The different systems of decision-making, the skills and methods emphasized by modern psychology, and many other helpful suggestions and insights adapted to the variables of a marital relationship are important. On the other hand, the humanistic view will insist on the qualities of a mature and liberated person and on developmental concepts of marital interaction. Nevertheless, these will never work without a conversion of heart and spiritual growth.

A dialogic spirituality in the light of the biblical word makes possible such conversion and growth. Spouses turn to each other and to God. In fact, God takes the initiative in calling husband and wife to dialogue, since both the spouses and God speak the same language of lovers.[39] Like worship, where God and his people engage in dialogue, the spouses "gift" one another in an oblative dialogue.

Depth of communication is the result of meaningful dialogue. The fire of communion in living and loving is maintained through the vehicles of communication: those of mind and body. To establish a relationship marked by the depth of communion of intimacy is a great challenge because it demands total freedom and spiritual nakedness. Furthermore, external pressures and internal ambiguities might compromise that experience of personal freedom. A possibility opens up through God's grace which calls us to true freedom. As Augustine said, "We are not free within ourselves, nor free from ourselves until we have encountered him who causes us to be born ourselves."[40]

Again, the narrative of God's activity, revelation, provides a model for dialogue of communion. Revelation, in fact, is personal communion in which God recreates the freedom and value of the person and makes possible the encounter with others and with God himself. The barriers of self-centeredness are overcome and communion becomes an ongoing reality. God is the ultimate possibility of communion for the couple who stand as the most telling metaphor of God's self-donation to the people.

Communication as communion occurs, therefore, only when the partners' relationship is characterized by an ongoing, free, and intimate relationship. The permanent call to communion breaks the emotional and mental restrictions of mutually alienating attitudes. The partners are free and open, and they give life to one another in the give and take of marriage. Finally, they create an interpersonal intimate living in which their lives are moved by one another. As real and intimate encounter, this type of communication as communion is worship.

Presence is a kind of personal communication in itself. To be together, even without much talk, strengthens a love relationship which, in turn, generates an atmosphere of communication. It can even nurture deep emotions because body language is the most original and basic human language.

Partners are eminently present to each other through their bond of love and commitment. On the one hand, their being present to each other in their daily interaction and human experiences is the essential part of their communication with the complex and rich variety of nonverbal communication. On the other hand, this presence is validated with words that speak their world vision, their desires and frustrations, dreams and joys.

This presence is salvific because the partners through their commitment participate in the concrete, loving intimacy of God's own person. This is at the core of marital spirituality.

The analogy to the mysterious presence of God's self-communication further deepens our understanding of this spirituality. The living dialogue with God in the ever-present revelation, and the marital love relationship, are both alive through the awareness of presence. Both realities are foremost a happening, but they are confirmed with words.

Present to each other, husband and wife encounter in their lives in a healing and supportive way, and they experience the challenges and demands of their journeying together. Enclosed mysteriously within the presence of God, marriage is actually the fertile ground of the true worship of self-sacrificing love and, therefore, of a true and unique spirituality.

Finally, communication is power because it is always a dynamic force, an ongoing reality which reveals and, at the same time, affects the person. "One of the greatest gifts God has given to spouses," says John G. Quesnell, "is the power to give life to one another. Through the medium of speech, spouses can communicate or destroy life in one another."[41]

Since this power is love generating through an intimate mutual understanding, especially through the quality of listening, it is the closest reality to total communication. But total communication, like complete knowledge of the other, is a lifetime task, never an actual reality. Hence, the challenge of this lost powerful human interaction.

The mystery of the inviolable interior space of the other already reveals a divine parenthood.[42] From the beginning God pronounces a word of life to establish a community of love. This word of life is not only creative from the beginning, but it permanently validates human existence as an ineffable power of salvation.

Translated into the art of communication, this theology of revelation creates a most important area of conjugal spirituality: communication as creative power toward perfection. So as the word of God demands faith and trust, communication in marriage is only possible in empathy and love. The spouses empower each other with deep and constant dialogue, as does the God of revelation whom they image in faithfulness. Their commitment to their union and to their fellow humans, if lived out in faith as self-gift of genuine communication, becomes a living sacrifice which worship celebrates.

## FAITH SHARING IN THE DOMESTIC CHURCH

Vatican II, referring to marriage and the family as a "domestic church," regained a rich biblical and patristic theology of the priestly dignity of the Christian couple.[43] This priestly dignity stems, not from the exercise of any sacred function, but from the natural sacramental character of their union, lived in the all-embracing nuptial mystery of Christ symbolized by the Christian couple. They meet the Holy through their human core and are empowered by the Holy through their covenant.

Another important vision which derives from that priestly dignity is the ministerial function of the laity as partners in the service of the church and as community builders. This vision, which is gradually being recovered, demonstrates the importance of the theological concept of the domestic church. From this perspective, not only does the couple learn its call to minister to their own concrete existence in the image of the church, but the ecclesial community develops the attitude of respect and mutuality of the family partnership from the model of the domestic church. In fact, the partnership of the family, which "is a living image and historical representation of the mystery of the Church,"[44] stands today as a most compelling metaphor of the church.

This new communal and sacramental perspective will enrich a theology of marriage and the family today, especially in the context of the contemporary crisis of traditional Christian values. The present, in fact, more than ever before, is strong in experiences, but weak in faith. From this perspective of the growth of the family as a living reality of the family of families (that is, the church), two different dimensions of the conjugal spirituality emerge: the inward family living within itself, and the outward faith witnessing beyond itself.

The inward family living in the "sanctuary of the Church in the home"[45] is spiritual if experienced as God's permanent free gift through the different inner components of its reality: a place where love, the law of family living, is experienced in its full and rich meaning; where humanization, identity, and the integration of human sexuality develop; where faith through the word is nurtured and shared, and, consequently, Christ is present; where prayer and contemplation are a reality; and where responsible parenthood and education lead into the integral reality of being human.

The outward faith witnessing depends on the same concept of the family as a living cell of a living organism. As such, the couple manifests the mystery of Christ which is present in its life and love. They make their actual experience visible, and so they become an extension of the church. As a community of hospitality, as a community witnessing to its faith in concrete experience, and as a community taking part in the building up of the church. The fostering of justice and peace, the humanization of culture, and especially the evangelization of society in the sphere of politics, economy, and science are essential tasks of the lay ministry.

The life of this small community of worship "receives a kind of consecration" which reaches and transforms all of its conjugal existence because it is called to be a presence and testimony to Christ's ministry which transforms all human reality. The spouses' profoundly humane and historical spirituality becomes a credible sign and instrument of salvation, as they "manifest to all people the Savior's living presence in the world, and the genuine nature of the Church."[46]

The theological analogy between church and family is not simply a useful pious comparison, but is deeply rooted in Christian tradition, both biblical and historical.

The New Testament tradition of the "domestic church"[47] is abundantly testified to in numerous references, and centers around the essential meaning of Christian marriage which describes and actualizes symbolically the transcendent mystery of Christ and his church (Eph 5:21-33). This central Pauline affirmation created a conjugal spirituality in the early church which viewed marriage as spiritual worship, donation, and service of the partners.

The early literature of the Church Fathers also has abundant references to the same analogy, especially John Chrysostom. His main point of departure is the idea of Christ's privileged presence in "the house of God" (the family), of which the wedding at Cana is a telling example in the light of the theology of John's Gospel. John Chrysostom sees the mystery of Christ and the church in the perspective of marriage as a "substantial image" and "a mysterious icon of the Church."[48] In Paul Evdokimov's words, "The grace of the priestly ministry of the husband and the grace of the priestly maternity of the wife form and shape the conjugal existence in the image of the Church."[49]

The historical tradition goes back to the very dawn of the Christian community and its worship, for at the beginning of Christianity "the Church meets in the house of" a Christian family.[50] Houses were not only literally churches (like Dura-Europos), but households gave birth to communities. The worshiping community, as distinct from the sacred temple gathering, originated in the bosom of the family, around the table, and under the couple's hospitality. They became a prophetic instrument of evangelization. The cases of Lydia and Cornelius are only two telling examples of decisive developments of nascent Christianity: the former represents the beginning of the expansion of the total church to Europe (Acts 16:14-15), and the latter is the first official acceptance of the Gentile world (Acts 10:1-23).

The theology of the domestic church constitutes, certainly, a sound vision of marriage and family spirituality, especially from the perspective of spiritual worship. As a metaphor of the total church, it struggles to live an analogous reality of caring and hospitality, of celebration and forgiveness, of prayer and peace, and of an unbroken unity in the midst of a broken society. In this family church, "where all the different aspects of the entire Church should be found,"[51] marriage is a concrete experience of Christian life in "faith working through love" (Gal 5:6).

\* \* \* \* \* \* \* \* \* \*

The theological understanding of the intimate faith sharing at home, like the understanding of the other important realities of agape-love, donation, and communication, provide the basis for the assertion of the existential and intrinsic relationship of marriage and worship at the core, not only of life, but of the Christian mystery itself. In specific Christian terms, the self-bestowal of the marital embrace and the sharing of one eucharistic cup and bread intersect in the mystery of the cross, the paradigm of Christian worship. Marriage can only be a vital and fulfilling reality of love when lived as a profoundly human and spiritually transcendent experience of spiritual worship in bed and board, children and society.

*Notes*

1. James F. White, *Introduction to Christian Worship* (Nashville: Abingdon, 1981) 25.

2. For a discussion of the importance of the analogical method and its application to theology and worship, see David Tracy, *The Analogical Imagination* (New York: Crossroad, 1981) 405-421.

3. L.L. Mitchell, *The Meaning of Ritual* (New York: Paulist Press, 1970) xii.

4. "For worship is an acknowledgement of Transcendence," she says in her classic study *Worship* (New York: Crossroad, 1936) 3.

5. In his existential vision M. Buber, *I and Thou* (New York: Ch. Scribner's Sons, 1970), insists on the dialogical structure of a human being which is the path to the absolute, and which links human beings necessarily to God. Marriage only radicalizes this human interpersonal reality and its transcendency.

6. Charles Davis, *Body as Spirit: The Nature of Religious Feeling* (New York: Seabury, 1976) 16.

7. Walter Kasper, *Theology of Christian Marriage* (New York: Seabury, 1980) 27. God's plan in Genesis is conceived in the light of Exodus: the mystery of man and woman in love is the symbol of God's covenant of grace, especially dramatized in the prophetic revelation (Hos 1:3; Jer 2:3, 31; Ez 16:1-14; Is 54:62).

8. See Tim 2:11; 1 Jn 4:9.

9. Especially in Paul's vision in the light of Exodus and Genesis, of Christ's bridal relationship to the church (Eph 5:21-33).

10. Ex 12:25, 26; 13:5; 19:5; Dt 10:12.

11. Jer 7:22-23; Hos 6:6; Dn 3:39-41; Ps 39:7-9; Ps 49.

12. See Eph 1:4-6; Phil 3:3; Heb 9:14.

13. *Sacramentarium Veronense*, nos. 1105-1110, ed. L.C. Mohlberg, Rerum Ecclesiasticarum Documenta 1 (Rome: Casa Editrice Herder, 1956) 139-140; *Le Sacramentaire grégorien*, ed. J. Deshusses, Spicilegium Friburgense 16 (Fribourg: Editions Universitaires Fribourg Suisse, 1971) nos. 838ff.

14. See. G. Martinez, "Marriage: Historical Developments and Future Alternatives," *The American Benedictine Review* 37 (1986) 376-382.

15. John Chrysostom (4th-5th century) is the best example of this theology, for instance, in his Homily 9 on 1 Timothy (PG 62:546ff).

16. R.P.A. Raes, *Le Marriage: Sa célébration et sa spiritualité dans les églises d'orient* (Belgium: Editions de Chevetogne, 1958) 12; see E. Schillebeeckx, *Marriage: Human Reality and Saving Mystery* (New York: Sheed and Ward, 1965) 344-356.

17. Says Y. Congar in his thorough study of the sacred in the Bible, especially in reference to Ephesians 2:14-15: "Jesus abolished definitely the separation between the sacred and the profane regarding people, places, and times" ("Situations du 'sacré' en regime chrétien," in *La Liturgie après Vatican II* [Paris: Les Editions du Cerf, 1967] 385-403).

18. Schillebeeckx, *Marriage* 12.

19. Davis, *Body as Spirit* 34.

20. See *Eucharisticum Mysterium* 3 and 6, in *Documents on the Liturgy (1963-1979): Conciliar, Papal and Curial Texts* (Collegeville: The Liturgical Press, 1982) 395.

21. See Karl Rahner, *Foundations of Christian Faith* (New York: Seabury, 1978) 116-133; Jon Nilson, "Theological Bases for a Marital Spirituality," *Studies in Formative Spirituality* 2 (1981) 401-413.

22. Erich Fromm, *To Have or to Be* (New York: Harper and Row, 1976) 44-47.

23. For the notion of the nuptial sacrifice of Christ, the author is dependent on P. Evdokimov, *The Sacrament of Love: The Nuptial Mystery in the Light of the Orthodox Tradition* (New York: St. Vladimir's Seminary Press, 1985) 122-123.

24. Loving another person means telling him or her: You will not die, according to the French philosopher Gabriel Marcel, quoted by Walter Kasper, *Theology of Christian Marriage* 22.

25. St. Augustine, *De Genesi ad Litteram* 9.7.2 (*Corpus Scriptorum Ecclesiasticorum Latinorum* 28/1, 275-276).

26. J. Ratzinger, "Zur Theologie der Ehe," in *Theologie der Ehe* (Regensburg and Göttingen, 1969) 102.

27. We are "sexed being," says Maurice Merleau-Ponty, *The Phenomenology of Perception* (New York: Humanities Press, 1962) 154-171.

28. Pope John Paul II, "The Nuptial Meaning of the Body," *Origins* 10 (1980) 303, quoted by Ch. A. Gallagher and others, *Embodied in Love: Sacramental Spirituality and Sexual Intimacy* (New York: Crossroad, 1984) 3.

29. See Erik Erikson, *Insight and Responsibility* (New York: Norton, 1964) 127-129.

30. Besides the biblical quotations in notes 10 and 11 above, see Exodus 10 (Yahweh is a passionate, committed lover), Psalm 139 (intimacy with God), and Song of Songs: 2:5-9; 3:2-5; 4:12-16; 6:3, 8; 8:6019; Teresa of Avila, *Interior Castle* and John of the Cross, *The Living Flame of Love.*

31. "Centuries of secularism have failed to transform eating into something strictly utilitarian. Food is still treated with reverence. A meal is still a rite—the last 'natural sacrament' of family and friendship" (Alexander Schmemann, *For the Life of the World: Sacraments and Orthodoxy* [New York: St. Vladimir's Seminary Press, 1973] 16).

32. René Latourelle, *Man and His Problems in the Light of Jesus Christ* (New York: Alba House, 1983) 243.

33. A.N. Greeley and M.G. Durkin, *How to Save the Catholic Church* (New York: King Penguin, 1984) 126.

34. Such as M. Krantzier, *Creative Marriage* (New York: McGraw-Hill, 1981), p. 37, who speaks of "marriages within a marriage" when he identifies six natural "passages" corresponding to first years, career, parents, middle and mature years of marriage. These change-patterns have to be taken seriously as "the signs of life" to be read in order to understand a proper spirituality of the family.

35. The author borrows this concept from P. Tillich and applies it

to marriage. "Every act of courage is a manifestation of the ground of being" (*The Courage to Be* [New York: Harper and Row, 1958] 181).

36. David M. Thomas, in one of the best synthesis of theology and secular values of marriage, warns against overemphasizing developmental concepts and undervaluing the need of a radical acceptance (*Christian Marriage* [Wilmington, DE: Michael Glazier, 1983] 119-120).

37. See Rom 12:1-3 and 1 Pt 2:5.

38. Buber, *I and Thou* 123-168; "Extended, the lines of relationships intersect in the eternal You" (p. 123).

39. See notes 10, 11, and 30 above.

40. St. Augustine, *Confessions* 10.27, 38. Paul and John's theology stress Christian call to freedom in Christ (Gal 5:1, 13; 4:26, 31; 1 Cor 7:22; 2 Cor 3:17; Jn 8:32, 36).

41. J. Quesnell, *Marriage: A Discovery Together* (Notre Dame: Fides/Claretian, 1974) 88.

42. Buber, *I and Thou* 123-168.

43. *Lumen Gentium* 11; see also *Gaudium et Spes* 47-52; *Apostolican Actuositatem* 2-10 (all translations of conciliar documents found in this chapter are from the Abbott edition), and especially *Familiaris Consortio* (On the Family) of John Paul II, 13, 55-58 ("Spouses are therefore the permanent reminder to the Church of what happened on the cross . . . Of this salvation event marriage, like every sacrament, is a memorial, actuation and prophecy"), no. 31, *Origins* 11 (1981) 437-466.

44. "In communion and co-responsibility for mission" are the words used to define relationships between ordained and nonordained ministries, which should prevent "continuous wavering between 'clericalism' and 'false democracy'" ("Vocation and Mission of the Laity Working Paper for the 1987 Synod of Bishops" 33-57, *Origins* 17 [1987] 11-14).

45. *Apostolicam Actuositatem* 11.

46. *Gaudium et Spes* 48.

47. See Rom 16:5; 1 Cor 16:19; Phlm 2; Col 5:15, among many other references.

48. *In Epistulam ad Colossenses* (PG 62:387), quoted by P. Evdokimov, *The Sacraments of Love* 139.

49. Ibid.

50. *He kat'oikon ekklesia* to designate house communities, or faithful gathering in a household, different from "the whole of the Christian movement," or "the household of God"; see E. Schillebeeckx, *The Church with a Human Face* (New York: Crossroad, 1985) 46-48; N. Provencher, "Vers une théologie de la famille: l'église domestique," *Eglise et théologie* 12 (1981) 9-34.

51. Pope Paul VI, *Evangelii Nuntiandi* 71, *Origins* 5 (1976) 459.

# 2

# Marriage as Communion: An Anthropological Vision

VIEWED FROM THE INSTITUTIONAL, INTERPERSONAL, OR RELIGIOUS standpoint, marriage is not a distinctively Christian phenomenon, but it is a human partnership with inherently religious symbolism. Consider the complexity of its dimensions: it is a personal bond consummated in a sexual relationship; yet its full human reality contains different levels of meaning which point to a transcendent mystery; it is secular and social and at the same time spiritual and personal. Philosophical anthropology and the phenomenology of religion explore these dimensions and stress the complexity of marriage. An entire range of questions stems from the nature and mystery of the conjugal bond as well as from the multiplicity of forms in which this human partnership has been realized in different historical periods and cultures.

Precisely because marriage actually takes place in a concrete historico-cultural context, theological reflection must recognize the complexity of this human experience, and this calls for interdisciplinary study. Theological anthropology sees a profound meaning in the created reality of marriage, for it recognizes therein the essential components of a community of love open toward God. An understanding of human values reveals how the experience of marriage touches the roots of people's lives; an understanding of redemption reveals how mar-

riage belongs to both the order of creation and the order of redemption. An anthropological approach is essential. "In good
theology one can no longer adopt the simplistic distinction between 'natural marriage' and 'sacramental marriage' . . ."[1]
Marriage is not only a meaningful sign of an anthropological
reality but also an expression of the human response toward
transcendence.

Furthermore, the lived experience of marriage in modern
society makes us more and more conscious of human existential needs, and theology has to interpret and respond to these
needs in correlation with the content of faith. Against the
background of the human sciences and our awareness of the
present historical reality, study of this complex experience that
is marriage calls for constructive reflection on its anthropological roots. That is where the sacramental mystery is anchored.
The crisis in the theological understanding of marriage stems
primarily from a crisis of culture, and new anthropological
perspectives can establish the possibility of a more personal
theology.

In fact, the underestimation of its human values or, more
precisely, the lack of a personalist anthropology and of an adequate theological consideration of sexuality has been at the
root of the weakness of the traditional approach to marriage.[2]
As Theodore Mackin puts it, "The marriage sacrament, like
all sacraments, has as its matrix a complex human experience. And there is no understanding of the sacrament unless
we first understand its matrix-experience."[3] In theological
terms, the covenant vision governs the partnership reality,
but that divine call without this created reality would be
meaningless. Although this chapter does not include all the
bases of the reality of marriage, such as the biological, psychological, or philosophical data, it will consider some basic
anthropological presuppositions concerning marriage from a
Christian perspective.

## THE ANTHROPOLOGICAL SHIFT

In the last decades the understanding of the content of faith
against the background of human sciences, especially anthropology, has meant a shift in cultural presuppositions from ex-

ternal and abstract conceptions derived from philosophical principles to a more personalist and existential vision of humanity and its destiny. Even before the council, theological investigation that was renewed through a return to the sources and a dialogue with modern sciences made a new theological anthropology possible.[4]

The mystery and contemplation of the person becomes a center of openness to the transcendent and a reflection of the divine; the body itself becomes a primordial symbol of wholeness in the sacramental reinterpretation of human experiences. If human sacramentality is a reality, our potential for a truly human, marital partnership is in itself a "natural" sacrament, because it is a meaningful sign of the human hunger for love, a hunger which points to God.

Theological anthropology seeks the full meaning of human existence, not in abstract metaphysical speculation, but in the concrete historical reality of the person open to transcendence. This fullness of meaning reaches its ultimate and most radical possibility in God becoming a person in the Incarnation. As the center of creation, the person lives in the mystery of the grace of God that urges him or her to full human potential and to transcendent destiny in the radical newness of Christ.

Rooted in biblical models and symbols, especially those in Genesis, this line of theological discourse opens up the possibility for a more realistic understanding of the profound structure of the human being. Christian vision draws inspiration from seeing the person as the image of God in all a person's relationships but especially in one's return to God. This has always provided a foundation and a coherence to Christian thinking, but today this vision has to be critically yet decidedly sensitive to cultural anthropology.

Early Christian writers drew inspiration from Hellenism: in their critical discourse they focused on the person as an ineffable mystery of openness to God. The "know-thyself" of Greek humanism became incorporated into an emphasis on the image of God as the mirror of human personhood. Later on, Augustine contributed neoplatonic influences, and in the Middle Ages Thomas Aquinas brought in Aristotle. The modern anthropological shift has meant a change from speculation concerning the static essence of human beings to an historical and dynamic perspective of the whole person, in the context of the Christocentric and eschatological horizon of the new humanity. Consequently, in the post-modern world, where all the efforts of theological and even anthropological and socio-cultural reflection center around the person and his or her crisis in present civilization, "all the pathways of the Church lead to man."[5]

This study of the person pursues three key aspects of the concrete and human reality of his or her salvation story: the person, the body, and the image of God.

The person in the fullest sense of the word is a singular being who chooses to be free (within the limitations of respect) in every actualization of his or her relation to the other. Such a person belongs to the new humanity as it is concretely realized in a community and celebrates the mystery of grace whenever human life is lived authentically. With inalienable autonomy, dignity, and rights, one becomes a true person in choosing, in relating to the other, and in living in a community. There is no authentic person in social and individualistic alienation but only in the encounter of a love partnership within the context of a caring community.

The body is not an object but a singular unified being where the spirit is. The Christian conception of the embodied spirit rejects any type of dualism or any kind of devaluation of the body and sexuality. "The body," in the words of J. Comblin, "is the foundation of the community, because it is the human being manifesting and communicating with others in a community."[6] The sexual character of the body is an essential dimension of the invitation to relate to others.

The mark of the creator is on the human person, who is brought forth from the primordial chaos by God's liberating love and covenant. God is the foundation and continuing presence of that interpersonal relation, that community of two which is male and female. The two can never find a complete wellspring for their community of love in themselves but only in the original source of agape, in God.

In Christian terms, the total person is his or her inability to overcome the experience of endemic alienation, division, and death, finds a new liberation in humanity become God in Christ. Through the mystery of the Incarnation, the old reality is transformed into the new person, capable of living the full value of freedom and love in solidarity with the other. Christ is the total splendor of the person as image of God.

The most challenging question a person must think about is how to articulate the feeling one has about oneself. If the question is existentially the same, the answer is always complex and open-ended because it is rooted in the depth of the mystery of the person, a unique individual who nevertheless needs dialogue with others. The deeper and transcendent meaning of the person cannot be found through science alone or even through reason alone because such meaning is fundamentally religious.

Among religions, anthropologies of individual or cosmic dualism are common. But biblical revelation rejects dualism and establishes the unconditional value of the total person as male and female, originating and intersecting in the creative act of God, agape (Genesis). Thus neither the individual person nor even the couple can find a total validation in themselves but only with God. In the relationship between God's mystery and the person's quest, a story of passion or meaning develops which only the language of love partnership can adequately describe. This story is articulated in the prophetic covenant.

From this background of the prophetic covenant, the concept of the person develops even further within the community of the New Testament. But the socio-cultural context and the vision of the church as institution, which has prevailed from the late Middle Ages, has prevented a deeper understanding of the personalist view of marriage in general and in ecclesial circles in particular. The search for the juridical essence of marriage predominated over the convenantal perspective found in Scripture and in the patristic writers. As for Christian anthropology, classical theology did not go beyond Boethius' definition of a person at the beginning of the Middle Ages.[7]

The modern dialogue between theology and contemporary culture has made it possible to develop a theology which considers the concept and complexity of the individual person with the seriousness it deserves. The person comes to be and is essentially enriched by the other, opening to and communicating one with the other in the encounter made possible by word and love. Among modern approaches to the different aspects of the human being, two philosophers in particular are especially significant as antecedents to a more personalist theology and, consequently, to a more personalist understanding of marriage: Ebner and Buber.

Ebner's spiritual search led him to the conviction that personal fulfillment and authenticity are possible only in the word-and-love dialogue of communion between two people and their relationship with the personal God. Word and love are the keys to a relational understanding of the person and his or her mystery. A living word constitutes human spirituality and makes the deepest of human encounters possible. There is no truly living word except the one of love, which liberates a human being and opens him or her to transcendence and to participation in God's love.

In his mystical and philosophical thinking, Buber strove to counter individualistic and impersonal conceptions of the person. He insisted on the relation of dialogue and reciprocity, the "I-Thou," by which a person is constituted and is present to the other. The other level of relation, the "I-It," only produces alienation because it reduces the person to an object of manipulation. The interpersonal relation of mutual self-revelation stems from God's calling the human being to existence and to a relationship of dialogue with him. "Extended, the lines of relationship intersect in the eternal You."[8]

Many other philosophers have provided breadth and depth of vision to a renewed horizon of the person; they have added a great variety of perspectives but have especially noted the importance of human freedom and love. E. Levinas, also inspired by biblical interpretation, voiced a strong reaction against modernity and its thirst for power. He insisted on the primacy of the relationship with the other and exhorted us to see in the symbolic epiphany of one's naked face both the indigent human condition and the transcendent divine.

From another point of view, G. Marcel spoke of the meaning of the human encounter made possible by fidelity and founded on a communion of love. Through the gift and interchange of love, a person becomes existentially fulfilled in that person's openness to the other. This love brings about union, not confusion. From an existentialist perspective, L. Lavelle says, in the communion with the other everyone receives the same life he or she tries to communicate to the other.[9]

When this interpersonal understanding of the person is applied to conjugal communion and sexuality, its theological relevance is obvious. It provides an intellectual grasp of human existence in the encounter with the other and in transcendence toward God, and this echoes the biblical notion of covenant as the basis of marriage. This also leads to a more profound understanding and better appreciation of the conjugal partnership and its sexual reality. It takes note of the totality of the human being, body and spirit, or it is by giving and receiving in one's totality that a person develops. In the words of Wilhelm Ernst, "the encounter of husband and wife in the love of the couple is, in the eyes of interpersonalism, the highest form of the I-Thou dialogue which constitutes the human being."[10]

This philosophy of "existence as dialogue" has influenced the anthropology of theologians like K. Barth and K. Rahner. It grounds and provides insights for a more personalist and less objectivist interpretation of the sacraments. In the case of matrimony, it reaches back to the existential roots of a person's experience and brings out the nature and quality of the marriage relationship. From the point of view of the person, we can draw some major conclusions regarding this relationship.

A person becomes truly such only in communion with the other and for the other, and thus is meant to attain his or her full complementarity and requisite mutuality in the conjugal community. With their solidarity in a common nature and basic needs, male and female are called to intimate coexistence, and this become a liberating and personalizing encounter. In fact, given the existential needs of the human person, one's aspirations toward fulfillment cannot be achieved except through interpersonal relations. That is the important message of personalist philosophy which was so often neglected in classical anthropology. Other human sciences, like psychology, confirm the fact that the need for others is the center of gravity of all human needs.[11] Although the ideal of interpersonal communion and the human need for others goes beyond the conjugal sphere, it is here that the spouses reach an integral actualization. The following comment that J. van de Wiele made in reference to the human person has its full confirmation in marriage: "To be a subject means . . . above all to come out of oneself in a movement without return, [and] that promotes the other, makes the other be, makes him/her to be personally creative."[12] This dynamic and personalist view has even greater importance in an age of rampant individualism, when only the individual is seen as "the basic building block of society."[13]

A person who is endowed with an inherent dignity and freedom is called to share his or her interiority and intimacy in a community of mutuality. Being equal but different, spouses are called to live within a relationship of freedom within and in relation to the other and to achieve a kind of balance therein.

Finally, the human person, this reality always new, this mystery in search of meaning, is called to a permanent commitment to fidelity. Here is where the greatest of personal freedom and of human frailty are most manifest. Every interpersonal relation shares the reality of death with the fears and ambiguities it creates in the present, and this challenges the mutual receiving and giving of commitment in marriage. The greatness of freedom is revealed because this freedom "is capable of overcoming the obstacles, and of renouncing . . . transitory values as needed to live in fidelity to one person."[14]

A dynamic view of the human person shows marriage as a journey with cycles or stages throughout life, stages which entail possible crises and make growth necessary. Psychological studies have increased our awareness in this regard, and rightly so, but overemphasis on developmental concepts, especially when borrowed from a competitive and pragmatic culture, can also devalue the dignity of the person. Because each person has absolute worth, he or she can never be viewed merely as the means for someone else's development. Marital growth is an essential part of life; yet it cannot be equated with success in all the qualities human beings may consider important. It is being faithful that constitutes a personal relationship, and in this sense marital growth also means growth in fidelity. In Christian terms, crises and challenges mean an opportunity of grace for the spouses journeying toward the agapic love design brought about by God's presence.

## THE SEXUAL PERSON

Openness toward others, which is part of the essential make-up of the person, is made concrete and actual in the sexual relationship. As Merleau-Ponty points out, the person is a unified being characterized by a sexually differentiated body; throughout the course of life and in one's whole personality, he or she is a "sexed being."[15] Sexual attraction and sexual desire are an integral part of each person and an essential means of communication between persons. Personal attachment, empowered by physical appeal, points toward a complete reintegration of love and commitment. This relationship should not remain at the peripheral level because it is meant to be personal in the deepest sense; it can represent concrete communication at its highest level, the giving of self envisioned in Christ's call to unity.

Sexuality, as a core of the conjugal community, is a powerful reality with complex meanings which have to be learned and cultivated. They are learned in the human process of personalization and psychosexual development through affective relations with others, and they enable the person to achieve a sense of identity, self-worth, and love.

These complex meanings make sexuality a powerful symbol of the human community. Fulfilled in personal intercourse, the sexual encounter is meant to convey the meanings of total validation and openness to and acceptance of the other. It either has a profound human significance or else becomes deceptive. This is because its dynamism tends essentially to lock two human beings in an all-embracing relationship. Sexual intercourse implies more than a matter-of-fact relationship remaining at a superficial level; sexuality configurates the person as embodied spirit in all his or her biological, psychological, and existential dimensions. Consequently, it is meant to move the person toward truthful and reciprocal acceptance and giving at the physical, emotional, and spiritual levels. Bernard Cooke states the link between the reality of human sexuality—the fact that we are a symbol in our very way of being and communicating—and the profound importance of sexual honesty:

> Our sexuality can reveal our relatedness to others, our accep-
> tance or rejection of them as equal human persons, our concern
> for and our interest in them . . . Sexuality can be a unique link
> between people; it can also be an immense barrier. It can com-
> municate love or hatred; it can provide great security for per-
> sons, or it can be a key symbol of one's self-depreciation. It can
> be used to establish and enrich intimacy among persons, or it
> can be used as a refuge from and substitute for real personal in-
> timacy.[16]

The symbolic reality of sexual intercourse makes possible
that creative freedom which characterizes true interpersonal
encounters. The corporeal condition is seen as no accident but
as something inseparable from the unity which is the person.
Though made possible by the flesh, sexuality depends more
on a caring relation of male and female, both limited and gifted, than on functional capacity. Sexuality is more something
we are than something we have. Human sexuality is not simply biological or corporeal; its deep meaning and potential
emerge mainly from an integral, personalist view of its erotic,
genital, and spiritual dimensions. This integral vision rejects
any spiritualistic or dualistic view of the person which deni-
grates the body or sexuality. Even more, it leads to the realization that only love can reveal the full meaning and value of
sexuality.

Perhaps the greatest challenge the person faces is the interpersonal relationship called for by the sexual dimension of
heterosexual love. Such an interaction is challenging because it
is marked by the paradoxical and complex need of total openness, and this can make the continuing and dynamic journey
with the other and for the other humanizing and meaningful.
The complex existential meaning of human sexuality calls for
the appreciation of all its dimensions.

In the aftermath of the sexual revolution, modern society experiences a crisis in the meaning of human sexuality. The symbolic and meaningful language of erotic energy is a powerful
yet vulnerable reality. Its very vulnerability points to how important it is to have a liberating and integrated representation
of the full meaning of sexuality, how it can advance the process of personalization and socialization. Though progress has
been made by the human sciences in the understanding of the

phenomenon of sex, this has not been accompanied by a personalist view of the human mystery and the total context of sexuality. For this reason, sex has been reduced, especially in the popular media, to genitality, a mere commodity in a consumeristic society. This presents a real challenge for the church called, as herald and servant, to celebrate the mystery of the whole person in marriage.

In regard to marriage, the most important task for the church is to integrate all human values and especially the full meaning of sexuality into a more personal theology. A personalist and existentialist theology will acknowledge marriage as a sacrament and recognize the importance of pastoral care. To be a welcoming and supportive environment of growth for couples, especially for newly-weds, the church must first have a positive view of sexuality. This will enable the church to serve as a model of intimate caring, a credible witness in the face of the emptiness created by post-modern culture. A positive view which embodies Christians ideals must be founded on the anthropological-biblical perspective. As J. Gevaert has rightly stated, Genesis provides "an acceptable and modern anthropology."[17] Being created "in the image of God" reveals the interpersonal nature of the man-woman structure. The archetypes presented by Genesis can still enlighten a modern person in search of authenticity and true freedom. Genesis illuminates two major foundational dimensions in particular: the meaning of sex and body and the meaning of the conjugal relation between the two sexes.

The Bible witnesses in a unique way to the quality and transcendence of human origins. The person is "the other," different from and yet in complete dependence on the creator; the only human answer to the challenge of life lies in liberating dialogue with God. God-created action is an action of covenant and liberation from the primeval chaos. There is union, fidelity, and communion in this created flow of life and goodness from the source, God agape. Humanity created in sexually differentiated bodies is a reflection and mirror of God's goodness; we image God in our very being as male and female. This prophetic vision leads to an open and positive appreciation of the body and sexuality; they are good because creation "was very good" (Gn 1:27-31). The whole of creation—

including sexuality—is seen as sacred, but it is not sacralized to the point of idolization.[18] It is also transcendent, but it is never exalted to the point of euphoric naiveté. While sexuality is sacred and transcendent in that the dynamic interpersonal relation of the couple which manifests the divine source, it is also only human and fragile because sexuality and mortality are linked together. Sexuality is thus seen as a gift from God in the service of love to form community between man and woman. Even after sin darkens the capability of love, the radical goodness of the gift remains the same (Gn 3).

The symbolic dynamics involved and what they imply about the interpersonal relationship of the couple are expressed in the biblical parable of the woman's origin. This simple Yahwist account (Gn 2:18-25) presents an answer to the human person's solitary loneliness; the foundation of the conjugal unity is seen in the two complementary poles of unerasable sexuality. Adam welcomes Eve as man's rib, as the answer to his innermost needs and desires. This has been rightly called "the first song of love." The established relationship is as important as the two differentiated sexes themselves because both individually and together, are God's image (Gn 1:26) and consequently of equal dignity in their mutual complementarity. They can only fully discover their individual identity in dialogue with the other and for the other. This is a differentiation of communion and togetherness, not of a dualistic brokenness and hostility, and therefore it rules out any dominance of one over the other.[19] But this joyful encounter becomes ambiguous when the male's supremacy is established (Gn 4:19-24). Despite the constant influence of biblical revelation, marriage tends toward sacralization, and some ambiguous attitudes toward sex prevail.

The Song of Songs celebrates human eroticism and love as a parable of the intimate love of God for the people. The couple image God's liberating creation and covenant in their faithful and creative love.[20] A sexual relationship of this sort is both humanizing and truly fulfilling.

Marriage "in the Lord" is a Christian sacrament. But here we speak not just in the narrow sense of the marriage ceremony but in the broader sense of the whole of conjugal life. This can only be properly understood from the order of creation. In the dynamic reality of conjugal love, the other person is embraced and the infinite human longing is fulfilled so that love conquers the fear and fact of death. But to speak more precisely, this fulfillment occurs "already, but not yet." In the perspective of Christian faith, there is an eschatological meaning to marriage, based on the salvific reality of natural marriage. As G. van der Leeuw wrote from the point of view of the phenomenology of religion: "The old primitive world knew marriage as a sacrament in the literal sense of the word. This implies that in some ways the end of marriage is not mutual comfort or procreation, but salvation to be found through it."[21]

The husband-wife relation, like the divine-human self-communication, can only exist in a relationship that corresponds to the archetype of original love presented by Genesis and characterized by true freedom, profound intimacy, and fidelity.

### Freedom

The first characteristic of conjugal love is freedom. People are free because they have the power to choose and shape their lives. In creating the meaning of one's life, a person should choose love because love best expresses those human values which are inseparably linked to human freedom and, in the process, delivers one from loneliness. Conjugal love must be more than just an escape; it requires mature emotional growth toward that authentic love which can be found in autonomous and stable relationships. Too often social conditioning, family dependency, and unconscious fears, originating from emotional scars or past and present anxiety, cripple the freedom of personal love. The challenge of conjugal love calls for personal decision; it presupposes a personality that is trying to be open to self-understanding and to understanding others.

Love is something we are called to be and to experience deeply. It is an actualization of the most important reality of our being and the heart of the conjugal encounter which seeks the sharing of the other. It is concerned for the well-being of the other, and promotes the growth of the other.[22] This kind of love is humanizing because it joins the two persons in a total relationship, an affective and effective union that results in mutual validation and meaning. Human love is never completely free and unconditional. Secondary and individualistic ends are inevitably part of the human experience of love, but they cannot be the main motivation if an authentic conjugal relationship is to develop. Love and freedom are inseparable in human experience, particularly in the most challenging of all, marriage. In fact, as J. Gevaert states, "love is the sacrament of freedom,"[23] because love is at the same time a "sign" of mature freedom and the place where freedom can grow.

In contrast with this vision of a true life-giving love in freedom, romanticized and idealistic love reduces a relationship to the sentimental and to unrealistic expectations. It is a false "sign" because it prevents that true freedom which can only come from an all-embracing acceptance of the real person in an intimate and interdependent relationship.

The experience of freedom and love points to the mystery of the inviolability and openness of the person and reveals both the greatness and fragility of human love. The personal journey that is marriage leads us to experience this at the deepest level. The greatness of human love stems from the potentiality for growth that it provides, for courage and generosity are engendered in an encounter of two freedoms won by love and fostered by love. To be authentically human, an encounter has to be free because, as Simon de Beavoir says, "authentic love should be founded on the reciprocal knowledge of two freedoms."[24] However, if freedom is the seal of authentic love, it is also the potential of its fragility. Awesome and ineffable though it might be, love is only human. Human unpredictability creates a positive tension to keep a relationship alive; love demands a continuing attitude of vigilance. Intimacy implies the total "nakedness" of two free people; to one another it creates the highest degree of personal vulnerability. This means love must be more than an occasional conquest; it can only be a life-time process, a process of self-giving. It is, in fact, a paradoxical dialectical process that makes both the individual freedom of each spouse and the positive dynamic of an intimate partnership possible.

Understanding the conjugal journey as an act of freedom makes love both a gift and a challenge and calls for a lifelong celebration, in Christian terms, a "marriage in the Lord." In fact, if the marriage celebration has to respect and build upon the foundational insights of a personalist view, the theology of this celebration must also incorporate the human experience of love and interpret its natural sacramentality in the light of the covenantal view of Scripture. Both the personalist and the biblical views converge in the mystery of the plenitude of freedom and love for which "Christ has set us free" (Gal 5:1).

## Intimacy

An integral view of the person shows us the depth and complexity of genuine intimacy. Our being is, in all reality, sexual; but intimacy cannot be reduced to sexual desire. Intimacy in marriage is meant to be the expression of love in the complete sense. It involves the physical and the passionate, but it also implies an attitude of unconditional love (*agape*) and the caring of friendship (*philia*). Consequently, conjugal intimacy is sexualized love reflecting the whole of a relationship, both the flesh and the spirit, pleasurable and responsible, communicative and creative.

The terms love and intimacy are ambiguous because their meaning is so often narrowed to only one of the components of the committed partnership: the physical, the affective, or the spiritual. Sexuality becomes a truthful symbolic language and a ritual of love only when love-making establishes an intimate bond in a meaningful manner. The sharing of the total self in the whole of a relationship culminates and is celebrated in the spontaneous way of corporeal communion through the irreducible power of eros. Rollo May's holistic view of eros is that "eros seeks union with the other person in delight and passion, and the procreating of new dimensions of experience which broaden and deepen the being of both persons."[25] This calls for not only physical but also emotional and spiritual nakedness. Committed couples describe this as "allowing themselves to be vulnerable." But they thereby validate one another's existence and bring bonding and intimacy into their relationship.[26] (And "risking the loss of self" by sharing the innermost self also holds true in our relationship with God.)

Nevertheless, spiritual love cannot always remove the barriers to intimate closeness because there is fear. Fear is a deception which can block one's ability to allow oneself to be wholly and deeply touched by the other. Fear takes different forms in different people; it may involve dependencies or even idealization. But each of us has innate capabilities for intimacy, and these can be developed through sharing, through mutual openness and trust, through personal reassurance. One needs a searching heart committed to a process of self-actualization by means of the twofold obligation in marriage: to accept and to give. The richness of conjugal love and its potential for growth are rooted precisely in this existential self-giving; as Teilhard de Chardin wrote: "Only those who are driven by passion love adequately, those who are led one by the other to a higher possession of their being."[27] This kind of loving self-gift, of self-sacrifice, in the true Christian sense, is in itself an openness to transcendence.

Our understanding of intimate sexual love would be incomplete without the inclusion of another essential dimension, namely, fruitfulness as an intrinsic gift and fulfillment of the sexual condition of the spouses. Love-making in the mutual self-giving and total possession of the union of intercourse is in itself a creative action which, by its natural meaning and dynamism, is oriented toward mutual enrichment and perpetuation in a third being. Anthropologists and psychologists have acknowledged this procreative component of the erotic state and order of being. As John F. Crosby points out, "Eros is the drive to create, to procreate, to communicate to another person in the most intimate way possible.[28]

Love, freedom, and intimacy are not only inseparable in an intimate partnership, they are also essentially linked to a sense of ethical responsibility toward the other and indeed toward all other human beings. Consequently, the ethical demands of procreative love call not only for fidelity to the other spouse but also for care of one's children, a vocation to life and generativity in general, and finally service geared toward the future of the community. The vocation of parenthood requires a real decision of personal conscience. As Vatican II says in reflecting on the equally important unitive and procreative meanings of marriage: "The parents themselves should ultimately make this judgment in the sight of God."[29]

## Fidelity

An intimate interpersonal relationship necessarily includes the dimension of fidelity. Freedom, intimacy, and fidelity are inseparable characteristics of a committed choice; they establish the two persons in one love, yet preserve the dignity of each inviolate. As a person cannot renounce his or her own dignity, a spouse cannot renounce commitment to a free, intimate, and faithful love without compromising the relationship.

Without fidelity, love is not an option of commitment to one another but only an unengaging action of affability or a simple transaction for a utilitarian purpose or common interest. Furthermore, faithful love demands commitment to a person— not to an idea, to a life style, or even to certain values. It is in fact a choice of loyalty, truthfulness, and concern for the sake of an inter-personal community. From a philosophical perspective, Gabriel Marcel described this kind of fidelity as the perpetuity of a creative testimony in the historical process, a creative fidelity which is required by the inexhaustible being of the person. Every egotistical retrenchment leads to a retrenchment of being both in the selfish one and in the other.[30]

Consequently, faithful love is an essential part of being human. It is an expression of our being which involves an open-ended process of radical commitment, always open to the mystery of an unpredictable person. It is a life-long journey of hope, because only when we hope can we love. In this sense, fidelity and love require and support each other—not in any forced sense but as essential parts of a process and a choice. In the many loving acts of ordinary conjugal interaction, fidelity and love are, in fact, dynamic and creative in the unfolding human pilgrimage. This orientation toward the future entails two qualities which are at the core of fidelity: unconditional love and a life-long commitment. Both are intrinsic demands of the conjugal covenant. As John Paul II states:

> The total physical self-giving would be a lie if it were not the sign and fruit of a total personal self-giving in which the whole person, including the personal dimension, is present: if the person were to withhold something or reserve the possibility of deciding otherwise in the future, by this very fact he or she would not be giving totally.[31]

Such emphasis on the total commitment that fidelity implies is even more important in our own time when marriages are failing at a very disturbing rate. Our contemporary culture is characterized by rapid social change, high mobility, and longer life expectancy. The many sociological factors that have fostered divorce are beyond the scope of this study. Here we can only point out once again the greatness and fragility of human freedom. But the Christian of the modern world has to live the ideal of faithfulness called for by the Kingdom. This ideal demands even more creative ways of maintaining integral fidelity and stability. Sexual exclusivity, meaningful communication, and an attitude of flexibility and adaptation are of course imperative. But even beyond these, there must be a process of realistic growth, of "many marriages within a marriage," to achieve life-time fidelity today.[32] Furthermore, stability, the fruit of fidelity, is needed in order to accomplish the task of raising a family successfully, especially the challenge of forming a community of persons who are able to love and serve. This kind of faithful love has a transcendent dimension because, more than any other expression of love, it images the unconditional love of God agape: a love that endures whatever comes, and does not come to an end (1 Cor 13:7-8).

\* \* \* \* \* \* \* \* \* \*

This chapter has attempted to elaborate on the new understanding of the person that Vatican II has provided and to show how this has resulted in a paradigm shift in the Christian vision of marriage. This new vision stresses the covenant significance of matrimony. It sees the essence of marriage as an intimate partnership from the center of love; it presents a positive view of sexuality, and stresses the dignity and freedom of the human person. The rational, juridical, and biological view of past centuries needs to be balanced with a deeper personalist understanding of the whole of the marital and intimate life, now envisioned as a community of persons. And with this balance the couple and the family will be better able to realize their vision within the larger community.

A man and a woman in love are called to be a sign of the ongoing manifestation of God to the people, and so the conjugal community is to be understood primarily as being ordered to human sharing in the divine goodness. A community of genuine mutual giving is a creative force. It not only provides the appropriate context for intimacy and reveals both the human and divine mystery; authentic marriage is also a living sign of salvation. It has human sacramentality at its very core and is a call to realize the saving mystery of Christ in our lives.

A more personalist approach to the complex and dynamic reality of this graced relationship will only enrich our current understanding of marriage. The human values we are called upon to actualize today in faith, together with the existential context of our times, point to the grounds for a modern theological synthesis of marriage. Our approach has to start from a biblical and genuinely anthropological understanding of the person as the place of the theophany of God. This reveals to us the deep transcendent mystery of marriage embedded in today's historical reality.

The human person is at the heart and center of it all. Precisely because marriage is a human reality and a natural sacrament with such various dimensions and complex intersecting meanings, our theological approach has to be interdisciplinary. Our method will involve critical interaction between biblical anthropology and Christian tradition; it will see marriage in the light of human sciences and the complex human experience of the couple. Such a personalist theology leads to a personalist sacramental vision of community; it sees us called (and gifted by that very calling) to live in "faith that makes its power felt through love" (Gal 5:6).

*Notes*

1. W. Ernst, "Marriage as Institution and the Contemporary Challenge to It," in *Contemporary Perspectives on Christian Marriage,* ed. R. Malone and J.R. Connery (Chicago: Loyola University Press, 1984) 69. The following studies are especially valuable in terms of an anthropological approach to Christian marriage: J. Ratzinger, "Zur Theologie der Ehe," in *Theologie der Ehe,* ed. H. Greven (Regensburg: Augsburg, 1972) 81-115; H. Doms, "Zweigeschlechtlichkeit und

Ehe," in *Mysterium Salutis*, ed. J. Feiner and M. Löhrer, vol. 2, 707-750; T. Mackin, "How to Understand the Sacrament of Marriage," in *Commitment to Partnership: Explorations of the Theology of Marriage*, ed. W.P. Roberts (New York: Paulist Press, 1987) 34-60.

2. Two major Catholic documents of the magisterium insist on the need for further theological reflection in terms of the personalistic reason behind the theology of marriage: Pope John Paul II, "The Apostolic Exhoration on the Family (see *Origins* 2 [1981] 438-467); *Gaudium et Spes* 47-51. "The beginning, the subject and the goal of social institutions is and must be the human person, which for its part and by its very nature stands completely in need of social life" (*Gaudium et Spes* 25). All translations of conciliar documents found in this chapter are from *The Documents of Vatican II*, ed. Walter M. Abbott (New York: Guild Press, 1966).

3. Mackin, "How to Understand" 34.

4. Two examples of this anthropological shift in theology are: K. Rahner, "Allgemeine Grundlegung der Protologie und theologischen Anthropologie," in *Mysterium Salutis*, vol. 4, 405-420; L.F. Ladaría, *Antropología Teológica* (Rome: Gregorian University, 1987).

5. Pope John Paul II, *Redemptoris Hominis* 14 (3-4-1979). See Charles M. Murphy, "The Church and Culture since Vatican II: On the Analogy of Faith and Art," *Theological Studies* 48 (1987) 317-331.

6. In his creative approach to anthropology from the perspective of Liberation Theology, *Antropologia Crista* (Petrópolis: Editora Vozes, 1985) 272.

7. "An individual substance of rational nature"; see Ch. Schultz, "Der Mensch als Person," in *Mysterium Salutis*, vol. 2, pp. 637-656.

8. M. Buber, *I and Thou* (New York: Ch. Scribner's Sons, 1970) 123.

9. L. Lavelle, *L'Erreur de Narcisse* (Paris: B. Grasset, 1939) 161. With regard to the phenomenological perspective of E. Levinas and its importance from the liturgical point of view, see Jean-François Lavigne, "A propos du statut de la liturgie dans la pensée d'Emmanuel Lévinas," *La Maison-Dieu* 169 (1987) 61-72.

10. Ernst, "Marriage as Institution" 64.

11. Erik H. Erikson, *Insight and Responsibility* (New York: W.W. Norton, 1964).

12. J. van de Wiele, "Intersubjectiviteit en zijnsparticipatie," *Tijdscrift voor filosofie* 27 (1965) 655, quoted by J. Gevaert, *El Problema del Hombre: Introductión a la Antropología Filosófica* (Salamanca: Sígueme, 1981) 66.

13. John Naisbitt, *Megatrends* (New York: Warner Books, 1984) 261.

14. Gevaert, *El Problema* 226.

15. P. Merleau-Ponty, *The Phenomenology of Perception* (New York: Humanities Press, 1962) 154-171.

16. B. Cooke, *Sacraments and Sacramentality* (Mystic, CT: Twenty-Third Publications, 1983) 52.

17. Gevaert, *El Problema* 114.

18. By "sacred" we mean that the whole of God's creation is holy by reason of its source. We affirm what E. Schillebeeckx says about the secular value marriage as given in the Old Testament; this stands in contrast with the rituals of the fertility gods, which attribute sexuality to the sphere of the divine. "Faith in Yahweh in effect 'desacralized,' or secularized, marriage—took it out of a purely religious sphere and set it squarely in the human, secular sphere" (*Marriage: Human Reality and Saving Mystery* [New York: Sheed and Ward, 1965] 12-13).

19. Two important articles from the theological and biblical point of view respectively: L. Bòff, "Visão ontológico-teológico de masculino e do feminino," *Convergência* 7 (1974); P. Grelot, "The Institution of Marriage: Its Evolution in the Old Testament," *Concilium* 55 (1970) 39-50.

20. For a critique of the theological evolution of marriage in Scripture, see the important research of J. Cottiaux, *La Sacralisation des mariages: de la Genèse aux incises matthéennes* (Paris: Editions du Cerf, 1982).

21. G. van der Leeuw, *Sakramentales Denken* (Kasel, 1959) 152. The following statement of Pope Leo XIII is relevant in this respect: "Since marriage is a divine institution, and, in a certain sense, was since the beginning a prefiguration of the Incarnation of Christ, a religious quality is an ingredient in it, a quality which is not adventitious, but inborn, but bestowed upon it by human beings, but built-in" (*Arcanum Divinae*, in *Acta Apostolicae Sedis* 12 [1879] 392).

22. Eric Fromm, *The Art of Loving* (New York: Harper & Row, 1956).

23. Gevaert, *El Problema* 214.

24. Simone de Beauvoir, *Le Deuxième Sexe*, vol. 2, *L'Expérience vécue* (Paris: Gallimard, 1960) 505, quoted by P.E. Charbon, *Amor e liberdade* (São Paulo: Herder, 1968).

25. Rollo May, *Love and Will* (New York: W.W. Norton, 1969) 74.

26. T.J. Tyrell, "Intimacy, Sexuality and Infatuation," in *Intimacy*, ed. A. Polcino (Whitinsville, MA: Affirmation Books, 1978) 55-70.

27. P. Teilhard de Chardin, *L'Energie humaine* (Paris: Seuil, 1962) 82.

28. John F. Crosby, *Illusion and Disillusion: The Self in Love and Marriage* (Belmont, CA: Wadsworth, 1985) 71.

29. *Gaudium et Spes* 50, see also 48.

30. G. Marcel, *Etre et avoir* (Paris: F. Aubier, 1935) 139ff.

31. Pope John Paul II, "The Apostolic Exhortation on the Family" (*Familiaris Consortio*), *Origins* 2 (1981) 441-442.

32. For a deepened understanding of the sacramental experience of marriage as process, see Bernard Cooke, "Indissolubility: Building Ideal or Existential Reality?" in *Commitment to Partnership* 64-75. From the sacramental point of view, John Meyendorff calls marriage a "passage" and an "open door" in *Marriage: An Orthodox Perspective* (New York: St. Vladimir's Seminary Press, 1984) 20. Concerning the ritual perspective of "passage," see Kenneth W. Stevenson, *To Join Together" The Rite of Marriage* (New York: Pueblo Publishing Co., 1987).

# THE TRADITION

# 3

# History and Its Lessons: Secular and Ecclesiastical Marriage

NEVER IN THE HISTORY OF WESTERN CULTURE HAS THE INSTITUTION of marriage been subjected to more radical and rapid changes than in the past two decades. Such profound crises have arisen in this complex human reality that some theorists have been led precipitously to decree "the end of marriage."[1] The new socio-cultural factors coupled with the modern explosion of human sciences and scientific discoveries are at the bottom of this moment of greatest challenge and hope.

For modern Catholicism, two documents of historical importance have emerged during the past twenty years: the redefinition of the concept of marriage from the biblical idea of the covenant (found in *Gaudium et Spes*); and the ensuing emphasis of personal values and insights of the behavioral sciences reflected in the new Canon Law.[2] Numerous interventions of the Magisterium and countless theological articles and books have attempted to tackle the problem of marriage in the Catholic Church. Since the problem is common to all Christian Churches, from an ecumenical perspective[3] marriage offers a unique opportunity for a common pastoral endeavor which has not yet been significantly explored. It is, in fact, one of the priorities of the pastoral agenda of all churches, and a main obstacle to Christian unity.[4]

The reality of marriage appears at a critical juncture today when it is seen in the background of the laborious development of the two thousand years of Christian tradition. This development represents two main stages. In the first millennium the church accepted the view of marriage as a secular reality originating in an act of human freedom and expressed in a multiplicity of concrete forms. The church, which viewed that secular reality as an experience of a saving mystery of love, applied a flexible praxis in a matter-of-fact manner. Weddings were only gradually introduced into the formal sphere and canonical power of the church from the eleventh century onward. This new stage preceded the development of the sacramental concept and the fully developed ecclesiastical definition of the institution of marriage.

## SECULAR MARRIAGE OF THE FIRST MILLENNIUM

In this first stage no Christian Church imposed any ritual celebration of marriage. The first millennium represented a gradual evolution toward an increasing intervention of the ecclesiastical hierarchy into the rite of marriage. This intervention was viewed as belonging exclusively in the context of pastoral care. From a pastoral concern of the bishops there emanated in the fourth century a liturgical prayer. This simple prayer did not substitute for the popular usages; the customary folk marriage celebration still belonged to the family and civil authority.

### "Christians marry like everybody else" (First to Third Century)

The liturgical documents are sparse in the pre-Constantine period. Although all the different rites of the sacramental signs are already attested at this time, there is no hint whatsoever of any sacred gesture or of any Christian prayer of marriage.

The references in the writing of the Apostolic Fathers in this matter point clearly in two directions: First, "Christians marry like everybody else" is quoted from the famous letter of Diognetes of this period.[5] The Synod of Elvira, held in Spain about

306, presumed the same practice.[6] Christians retained the customary practices of their own culture while subjecting themselves to the formulas of Roman legislation.

The second direction made transparent through the documentation of the early church was as important and clear as the first: Christians received their inspiration for their marriage life from the Pauline doctrine. The Apostle indicated that the marriage covenant must be experienced "in the Lord."[7] Certain elements of polytheistic religion, like idolatrous sacrifices or licentious folk traditions, were avoided by the Christian spirit. Tertullian opposed the common pagan usage of the crowning of the bride with flowers, as well as any mixed marriage with a pagan. To marry a pagan meant to be idolatrously crowned with him, and led into idolatry.[8]

The Church of Antioch offered the first attested case of the intervention of the bishop into the reality of marriage. Bishop Ignatius wrote to Polycarp at the time of the Emperor Trajan, between 98 and 117: "It is fitting that men and women who want to marry get the approval of the bishop, so that their marriage is according to the Lord, not according to passion."[9] This important testimony was simply a pastoral admonition and a rather isolated case at the time. From the liturgical or the canonical point of view, the bishop's approval had no bearing whatsoever. The *nubere in Domino*, to which Clement of Alexandria[10] also alluded at the end of the second century, pointed to the Christian consecration and the ecclesial character of marriage. This consecration and character stemmed from one's salvific initiation into the church at baptism. No explicit intervention of the Christian community was wanted in an affair that belongs to the exclusive sphere of a family.

## Ritual Symbols of Greco-Roman Marriage

The study of the popular folk rituals of marriage in the Greco-Roman world provides us with the cultural and symbolic background from which the western forms emerged.[11] Particulars of those rituals are well known.[12] They are relevant here as long as they help to understand an historical process, and the consciousness and stance of the church regarding that process.

As far as engagement is concerned, there are some main differences between marriage in Greece and in Rome which are necessary to examine specifically. In Rome the engagement was celebrated with special rites, at least from the third century, and played an important role from a juridical point of view.[13] On the contrary, the Greek and other laws, like Semitic, Germanic, and Celtic, did not have a distinct customary rite of engagement.[14] Here the reciprocal formal consent and conjugal union involved several ritual acts through different stages during the nuptial celebration. Nevertheless, similar essential rites formed the institutional elements of marriage across the Empire.

In Rome the presentation of the bride took place in the paternal household where the engaged couple exchanged their formal consent. The witnesses signed the contract on the *tabulae nuptiales*. Immediately afterwards, the *pronuba*, maid of honor, led the wife to the husband, and the *dexterarum iunctio*, the shaking of the hands, took place. This essential gesture represented the climax of the marriage ceremony in Rome. A sacrifice to the household divinities preceded the wedding banquet. For the new wife, moving to the husband's household (*deductio in domum*), meant an initiation into a new religion—the religion of the husband.[15]

It is important to point out other gestures that received universal acceptance within western culture. The nuptial ring given by the groom to the bride, the dowry, and the more recently introduced mutual kiss, were in Rome integral parts of the wedding ceremony.[16] It was also customary for the wife to dress in vestal white (*tunica recta*), and a purple veil (*flammeum*) with a wreath of flowers covering her head.[17] Other archaic wedding forms survived in certain regions. The most common was the *confarreatio* in which the spouses presented to the god, Jupiter, the offering of a type of hard wheat nuptial loaf.

Beyond all these legal and ritual ceremonies, in the later period of the Empire a type of "free marriage" appeared to be popular, especially among lower classes. This marriage was based on the mutual consent of the spouses. The Christian Emperor Justinian (527-562) sanctioned these "common law" marriages, stating that "nuptias non concubitus sed consensus facit,"[18] that is to say, the conjugal pact was not formalized by the sexual act (*usus*), but by the consent (*consensus*). In this case, the affective and effective will of the spouses to start a new community was validated, and the formal ritual usages over- looked. This was the result of a process of secularization prac- ticed in the Christian Roman Empire.[19] The *Lex Romana Uticen- sis* of the ninth century supported the notion of the free consent of the partners as the primary element of marriage, with the condition that the consent be given in the presence of witnesses.[20]

This summary of essential ritual symbols presented so far highlights the primary role of religion in the traditional mar- riage known by Christians of the first three centuries. In fact, the household divinities (the *lares*, the *penates*, and the *manes*) constituted the foundational dimension of the institution of marriage and family, as *nuptiae sunt divini juris et humani communicatio*.[21]

The partners' consent and the pact between two families provided the grounds for the sacred initiation of the woman into the secret rites of new household gods by the husband- priest (the new *pater-familias*). "In the case of both the Greeks and the Romans," writes E. Schillebeeckx, "marriage was not originally based on interpersonal relationship. Nor was it based directly on the procreative act, leading to the founda- tion of a family, or on marital and paternal authority, but on the 'religion of the hearth,' the *focus patruus*."[22] The ritual sym- bols emerged from their polytheistic religious consciousness to express the indissoluble union of the partners through the communion with the divinities.

Early institutional Christianity assimilated this basic anthro- pological reality and created a new religious synthesis. Chris- tians accepted the basic cultural and symbolic patterns with a new religious context and inspiration centered in Christ as the symbolic *"Pronubo."* This was realized within a staunch mon- otheism and a conservative moral code. The natural conflict between the household divinities versus the God of the cove- nant was minimized by the fact that most couples converted *after* their marriage. Within a process of general secularization of social and family institutions that took place in the Roman Empire with the pretorian legislation, the outset of Christianity gradually developed a reinterpretation of the symbolic gestures of the marriage initiation, as documented already at the beginning of the post-Constantine period.[23]

### Formation of a Liturgy of Marriage (Fourth to Eleventh Century)

The fourth century marked the beginning of an intense period of liturgical creativity. From that century onward the first vestiges of a liturgy of marriage are documented. The first liturgical formularies appeared as a result of a progressive intervention of the bishop at the nuptial celebrations. The prayers on the occasion of a marriage covenant did not represent a ritual marriage as such, nor did the pastoral care have any canonical jurisdiction. A juxtaposition of familial and popular customs formed the basically secular celebration of the marriage of Christians. The simple gesture of liturgical blessing with the mutual consent of the partners during the wedding within a household setting merely demonstrated the spiritual solicitude of the church.

Before citing the Roman sources, it is important to note an earlier comment by Tertullian (c. 160 - c. 240) in his work *Ad Uxorem*:

> How shall we ever be able adequately to describe the happiness of that marriage which the Church founds, and the Eucharist confirms, upon which the prayer of thanksgiving sets a seal, which angels praise, and to which the Father gives His consent? For not even on earth do children marry properly and legally without their fathers' permission.[24]

Some historians see here an indisputable reference to an existing liturgy of marriage integrated into the celebration of the eucharist. On the contrary, this text is correctly understood only if it is interpreted within the context of an exhortation to shun any contract of marriage with a pagan. The right interpretation of the key words of this text of the Catholic period of Tertullian is crucial. Marriage must be according to the Lord; Christ is the foundation of marriage through the all-embracing mystery of the church (*ecclesia conciliat*). Contracted between two baptized people, marriage receives its confirmation in the eucharist (*confirmat oblatio*). Tertullian does not refer to a liturgical ritual blessing, but to a liturgy of thanksgiving of psalms and hymns (*obsignat benedictio*). He alludes also to the blessing of assent by God the Father (*pater rato habet*).

The African writer presents the theological implications and the Christian character of marital covenant *in nomine Domini*. The covenant becomes a sacrament by virtue of the faith actualized within the participation of a eucharistic community.[25]

The second half of the fourth century marked the stage of an already nascent nuptial liturgy. The leaflets compiled in the sacramentary of Verona (fifth-sixth centuries) attested the first formulary: *Incipit Velatio Nuptialis.*[26] It provided the prayers for the Mass and the solemn prayer of blessing of the wife. The subsequent Roman sacramentaries, the Gelasian (seventh-eighth century) and the Gregorian (seventh-eighth century), reproduced basically the same liturgical content. These liturgical formularies presented likewise the first hints of a liturgical theology of marriage. There were no rubrics confirming customary ceremonies in the church.

At the time of Pope Damasus (366-384), there was already evidence of a liturgical rite in Rome and in Italy. This rite was reserved for the first-time married and consisted of a special blessing for the couple by the priest at the moment of the veiling of the bride before the altar.[27] Ambrose of Milan (374-397) attested the same veiling ceremony in Milan. The first detailed description of the *velatio nuptialis*, priestly prayer and veiling of the couple, is found in Poem 25 of Paulinus of Nola (353-431).[28] This veiling, performed by a bishop in the province of Rome, was already synonymous with the nuptial blessing. In this first step of development, which lasted for the first millennium, the trend favored the adoption of the Roman veiling and blessing in the context of a Mass. These were to be enacted immediately after the Our Father. The *Praedestinatus* written at the time of Pope Sixtus (432-440)[29] attested to the beginning of this new trend. Marriage still belonged to the civil jurisdiction and was contracted under its authority. The church assumed secular practices, conferring on them a redemptive symbolism, which consecrated a human reality essentially founded in the order of creation.

Diversity, stemming from regional cultures or local customs, still inspired a variety of local rites. In northern Africa at the time of St. Augustine the *Tabulae nuptiales*, or marriage

contract, was signed by the bishop.[30] In Gaul and Spain the ecclesiastical intervention was characterized by the *benedictio thalami,* or the blessing of the nuptial chamber.[31] Once again, an
ancient practice rooted in a pagan fertility rite provided the
cultural background of a liturgical framework.

In England the wedding ceremony also revolved around the
blessing of the nuptial chamber, apparently a common feature
to the archaic Gallican traditions. In fact, the so-called Benedictional of Robert, an Archbishop of York, provides several
formularies in that respect.[32] The topic of one of those prayers
is the wedding ring, which indicates the importance attached
to its Christianized symbolism. Liturgical documentation does
not transmit other specific vestiges of the Celtic rites of the
early Middle Ages. In any case, the primitive rituals did not
include the eucharistic celebration. This use of a eucharistic
celebration was adopted under the influence of the Roman liturgy, and passed along by the monks. Beginning with the Pontifical of Durham (at the end of the ninth century), and extending into the tenth and eleventh centuries, the formularies fit
into three categories: a Mass of marriage, blessing of the nuptial chamber only, or both.[33]

In Germany, on the other hand, the rituals depended on the
influence of the Roman liturgy for the entire first millennium.
In contrast, the Sacramentary of Fulda (tenth century) of Visi-
goth origin, was a new example of juxtaposition of local traditions which remained independent of Rome.[34] The Norman influence was attested by the practice of the *benedicio thalami* a
century later.

Through the lower Middle Ages the marriage of Christians
remained basically a family feast and a secular reality. The
customary rituals that stemmed from the ancestral cultural
background were Christianized by adding new symbolic
meaning. The mutual consent among families and spouses
was always considered the essential element. Whereas the
veiling in Rome and Italy was the characteristic liturgical ritual, in the rest of the western countries the introduction into the
bridal chamber represented the sole moment of priestly intervention through prayer. However, after the seventh century
the veiling became in most countries the eminent sign of
priestly intervention. This would happen under the influence

of the Church of Rome in the Frankish and Carolingian periods. In both cases the liturgical action was considered only facultative. The marriage rituals, already a fact, were obligatory in the case of a marriage of minor clerics. On the contrary, legitimate second marriages were excluded from the veiling and blessing ritual, as well as those couples who had been living together, or were not in good public standing. The marriage celebration was liturgical and religious; no canonical or ecclesiastical discipline was involved at this time.

In the East the nuptial liturgy developed faster and ran parallel to a profound theology of marriage. On one hand, the Greek Fathers expounded the reality of marriage from an eminently spiritual perspective. This perspective was inspired in the Pauline theology of a Christ-church, husband-wife conception. On the other hand, the rapid development and legal validity of rituals were due to the direct intervention of the Byzantine emperors (eighth-eleventh centuries). In fact, starting with Leo III (717-740), the intervention of the priest with the liturgical rite constituted the canonical form of valid marriages.

The composition of formularies and the first expression of a specific Christian ritual of marriage date from the fourth century. Here again, the link between the traditional cultural background and the new symbolic ritual is clear. Christians adopted the main element of marriage folk rituals, the *ekdosis* (handing over of the bride). This was performed in Greece by the bride's father, who put a garland of flowers on the head of each of the engaged. The church opposed the garlanding at the beginning, but soon adopted the practice, while providing it with a new meaning. Garlanding became the foundational symbolic rite of Christian marriage. Garlanding, the *stephanoma*, was in the east what the veiling was in Rome. The priest soon assumed within the community the traditional role of the father within the family rituals.

Beginning with John Chrysostom (fourth-fifth centuries) this ancestral rite of pagan Greece was given a profound Christian significance: "A garland is placed on their [spouses'] heads as a symbol of their victory, because they reach victorious toward the port of marriage, without ever having been vanquished by pleasure."[35]

Garlanding by the priest was already practiced in some

churches at the time of Gregory of Nazianzen (second half of fourth century). Gregory indicated that the garlanding was more appropriately performed by the priest than by the father of the girl.[36] Its liturgical character appeared clearly in Armenia in the fourth century. It was attested to by the formulation of the blessing and the liturgical hymns of that period. The priest was to bless the garlands and to place them over the heads of the bride and groom.[37] This Armenian practice became an ecclesiastical tradition adopted by the other churches of the orient from Constantinople to Alexandria, particularly from the time of the patriarch Narses I the Great (363-372).

The whole rite of the *ekdosis*, previously described, whose culminating moment was the *stephanoma*, was thus transferred from the secular to the ecclesiastical sphere. Unlike the west, in the east, from the beginning of the eighth century, a canonical jurisdiction was accepted by *Novelle* 74 of Leo VI (886-912) gave the church's rite a juridical validity that made marriage legally indissoluble.[38] This legislation was developed more completely with The Golden Bull of the Emperor Alexius (1081-1118). Thus the *stephanoma* became the constituting act of marriage from a canonical and sacramental point of view. Second marriages were excluded from this specific marriage rite and blessing, as was the case in Rome with the veiling.

Regarding the eucharistic celebration, the practice was not constant in all Eastern Churches. In Alexandria it appeared in the fourth century. The Mass was celebrated in the house of the bride, where the priest assumed the role of the father in handing the girl over to the bridegroom.[39] On the contrary, the Greek-Byzantine liturgy, later in the tenth century, was customarily a rite of communion, the *Missa Praesanctificatorum*.

The Eastern Churches were a century ahead of the Latin regarding the incorporation of civil marriage into the church's liturgy. But this incorporation did not mean, as in the European high Middle Ages, an exclusive ecclesiastical affair, since the civil marriage contract was also considered valid. Although the canons that regulate marriage were already completed in the twelfth century, their mystical inspiration avoided the pitfalls of legalism. The priest here became the only minister of the sacrament through his solemn blessing and the act of garlanding.

In regard to remarriage, no solemn blessing was granted in either Latin or Greek Churches for those in a second marriage, even after the death of the first partner. During the first millennium pastoral flexibility and a relative pluralism in interpreting Scripture and tradition prevailed in regard to the evangelical ideal of the marriage bond. The church followed, in many instances, the practice of leniency and tolerance that characterized most patristic writings in readmitting those remarried after divorce to the eucharist. The prerequisite for readmittance was to practice penance.[40]

## ECCLESIASTICAL MARRIAGE

In the Latin Churches marriage remained until the ninth century a civil and familial ceremony. From this century until the Council of Trent the last phase of evolution opened up the gradual takeover of the discipline of marriage and the regulations of its ceremonies by the authority of the church. Those ceremonies were transferred first to the front of the entrance to the church (*in facie ecclesiae*), and later to the assembly in the church. Consent remained the essential element, but now the priest received that consent after a public pre-nuptial investigation. By imposing a new sacred and ecclesiastical model, the hierarchy aimed to counter the abusive public customs of the "Dark Ages" within a wider movement toward a new social order.

### Marriage "in facie ecclesiae" (Ninth to Thirteenth Century)

Pope Nicholas I (d. 867) offered an account of the ritual of marriage for his time: the spouses presented an offering and participated in the eucharist on the day of the transfer of the bride to the groom's house. Although the statement of Nicholas regarding the moral obligation of the ritual blessing and crowning has been interpreted differently, the main assertion of the pope in his Letter to the Bulgars was that "the only condition of a genuine marriage is the consent of those who get married."[41] His statement was intended only to be a reminder of the validity of the classic Roman law and an interpretation of tradition. Thus marriage did not belong to the forum of the church, and the marriage ritual was not compulsory.

Nevertheless, the socio-political conditions of Western Europe in the aftermath of Charlemagne's death (814) led to a progressive intervention of popes and bishops into civil institutions. The decretals of Pseudo-Isidore, commonly dated from the year 845 but falsely attributed until the Renaissance to popes and councils of the ancient church, marked the beginning of this new ecclesiastical interference.[42]

The church's takeover did not stem from a need to appropriate the civil jurisdiction of the marriage contract, but from a general breakdown of social institutions and especially of the common law that regulated marriages. The balance between the ecclesiastical and secular powers shifted dramatically at the outset of the birth of Europe. The bishops, representatives themselves of the feudal power, intended to confront the practice of abduction, the repudiation of the wife, and clandestinity in marriage consent. Regarding clandestine marriages, that is, those based simply on a private agreement between two individuals, the church was particularly concerned in requiring the public legal form of marriage.

The anonymous Pseudo-Isidorian Decretals and other canonical writings of this epoch established the legitimacy of marriage on the grounds of public inquiry and legal form. To the mutual consent and the local traditions of the past was added an ecclesiastical solemnization which became obligatory. This process of the transfer of jurisdiction, and consequently of sacralization of a secular marriage, initiated decisively at the end of the first millennium, lasted until the Reformation and the Tridentine canons. It did not immediately affect the lower classes, and in some European regions, like Tuscany in Italy until the fifteenth century, secular archaic forms of marriage were still accepted by the church.[43]

The Pseudo-Isidorian Decretals, aimed at a disciplinary and moral reform, established the ecclesiastical impediments, particularly the crime of abduction, and protected the indissolubility of marriage contracts. Civil marriage became ecclesiastical marriage, since church law imposed the terms of a celebration: previous inquiry, dowry, public contract and consent sanctioned in the church by the priest. Later, the *Decretum Gratiani* (canonical collection of c. 1150), gathering different canonical sources, confirmed this trend and made compulsory the liturgical celebration. Its main elements, centering around the mutual consent, made the canonical contract legitimate. The priest was the substitute in many instances for not only the *pater-familias,* but also for the justice of the peace. A more strict and uniform practice of understanding the indissolubility of marriage prevailed.[44]

The jurisdictional authority of the church was perfected in Europe between the eleventh and thirteenth centuries. Within this new ecclesiastical form the *Ordines ad facienda sponsalia* (rituals) developed. A typical example of the ritual is found in the sacramentary of Rennes (Brittany), dating from the twelfth century. It is a classic example of a marriage before the front door of the church (*in facie ecclesiae*). The gathering went into the church only for the eucharistic celebration and the blessing. These rituals had previously formed the classic Christian Roman marriages and were restricted to the sacramental function. This and other Anglo-Norman sacramentaries constitute a transitional stage from the simplicity of the early Roman sacramentaries to a complete liturgical and canonical rite of marriage. The local traditions still varied, but the essential element, from the twelfth century, remained the same: "the formal and public manifestation of the nuptial consent before the assembly" (*in facie ecclesiae*).[45]

## Reform (Sixteenth Century)

With the definitive transfer of the nuptial ceremonies from the home to the church, the canonical and ecclesiastical character of the marriage institution developed. Parallel to this, scholastic theology developed the ontological and specific nature of the sacramental sign. Consequently, the sacramental reality of marriage was examined, as well as the constitutive and specific element of marriage itself.[46]

Prior to the Council of Trent, different liturgical, canonical, and theological trends intertwined. A conceptual and juridical perspective prevailed at the expense of a vision of the mystery and the biblical inspiration predominant in the patristic period. Augustine was the main inspiration of the medieval theology. He saw marriage as the *sacramentum-signum* of the great mystery of the union of Christ and the church. Hence, marriage was thought of as indissoluble.[47] The scholastic theology affirmed its objective indissolubility, which corresponded to that symbolism based on an ontological conception of the nature of the sacrament.

The theologians of Trent ratified the Augustinian conception, which has prevailed from Trent until the present.[48] Catholic theology overlooked, in the following centuries, the mystical and biblical inspiration of Christian marriage. Canon Law and the Tridentine ritual remained the basis of theological and pastoral thinking. Hence the Catholic mentality of marriage became dogmatic and legalistic, and an inflexible praxis of indissolubility was adopted.

The *Ordines ad facienda sponsalia*, the rituals of the high Middle Ages, constituted the background of the Tridentine reform. An imbalance in the liturgical theology of marriage was already noticeable. The concern was predominantly canonical and ethical, whereas in the early centuries the Roman sacramentaries had provided a biblical theology and spirituality. For instance, the *Veronense* and *Gelasianum* presented a solid doctrine based on Genesis 2:18-25. The *Gregorianum* took inspiration from the Pauline doctrine of Ephesians 5:21-33.[49] This last biblical reference appeared as a pericope for the first time in the lectionary of Murbach, and was included in the Roman Missal of 1570.

From the strictly liturgical point of view, the pre-Tridentine period presented in France three types of rituals. These rituals were based on the formulations of consent and with two different ritual parts. The main change stemmed from juridical substitution of the father of the family by the priest, and most of the thirteenth- and fourteenth-century rituals substantiated that fact. The old *traditio puellae*, the giving away of the bride, consequently lost its original significance, and the spouses took a more active role through the *dexterarum junctio*, the joining of hands.

The Council of Trent (1545-1563) definitively consecrated the clericalization of the nuptial rite. This was particularly evident in the formula from the fourteenth century, with which the priest effected the bond: "Ego vos in matrimonium coniungo, in nomine Patris . . ." Although the council was flexible in regard to other local usages, it established some common norms: three inquiries in church before the celebration, and the presence of two witnesses at the ceremony. Nevertheless, the main concern surfaced in the decree of *Tametsi* (1563) regarding clandestine marriages, which were illicit but valid if contracted freely.[50]

This council did not represent any important stage in the evolution of the rite, but it did initiate a new legal form. It aimed at laying the social ground work for the validity of the sacrament. A similar canonical attempt had been made at the Council of Lateran IV (1215) against "clandestine" marriage celebrated at home without the priest.

The statement of Trent regarding theological, liturgical, and canonical matters consecrated the tradition, developed during the high Middle Ages, of marriage as one of the seven sacraments. These statements confronted the challenges posed by the reformers. Such challenges included emphasizing the order of creation and the natural reality of marriage, denying its sacramentality in the order of redemption, challenging the competence of the ecclesiastical authority concerning its validity, and considering the possibility of divorce.

The Ritual of Paul V (1614), the first official Roman ritual, reflected the same concern for the validity of the marriage contract. It represented a marriage rite strongly juridical, with liturgical expressions of a specific theology of marriage minimalized. Rome pursued the codification of common usages in different European regions at the time. Pluralism under ecclesiastical hierarchy was respected, but the trend toward a unification of the rite had been established.

## LESSONS OF HISTORY
## AND THE FUTURE OF MARRIAGE

Historical theology provides an essential perspective in rethinking the present situation. On the one hand, history shows the connatural plasticity of marriage in its multiple forms and thus its cultural reality. On the other hand, permanent human values in which the Christian mystery is embodied surface from that historical perspective. Thus its foundation is lasting truth. The dynamic relationship between church and marriage has always been an unfinished process and remains so today. This era of Christianity after Christendom is radically different from the past, and demands a new integration of the celebration and the living of conjugal love into the Christian mystery.

## Vatican II Reform

With the Renaissance and its process of secularization, which was intensified with the Enlightenment, the first conflicts for the control of the marriage institution arose. The modern secular states reasserted their judicial authority in the case of civil marriage. Furthermore, the secularist philosophies and political systems represented a great challenge to the traditional Christian view of marriage and family.

The Vatican Council faced these challenges in three main decrees: *Sacrosanctum Concilium, Lumen Gentium,* and especially *Gaudium et Spes.*[51] Marriage is seen in these documents within the biblical theology of the covenant and personal perspective. It is defined as a personal community within which the partners give and accept each other (covenant), and also as an intimate partnership of marital life and love (personal perspective). This Christian understanding of conjugal and familial life is essential from a theological and ethical point of view. The perspective was consequently broadened, not only retracing the biblical meaning, but also with the help of modern human sciences. The theology of these documents represents a reaction against a contractual mentality, which, taking inspiration from canonical sources, had narrowly stressed the objective and natural components while ignoring the personal dimension of marriage.

The liturgical constitution *Sacrosanctum Concilium* pays great attention to this sacrament. The document demands a restructuring and enrichment of the rite; it considers the different developments of history as progress, and aims at correcting the incongruities of the past which the Tridentine decrees did not solve. The liturgical movement prior to the Vatican Council had already provided national models: Germany, 1950; Belgium, 1958; Canada, 1964. In comparison with the Tridentine ritual of 1614, the new marriage rite represents progress. A new sacramental theology makes its appearance in the Introduction. The new ritual has a biblical foundation which inspires its perspective and content. Marriage is seen not from a simplistic contractual approach, but from the breadth of the covenantal mystery of salvation and in concrete relation to the eucharist. It is viewed as a basic sacrament in the order of creation and a paradigmatic sign of the mystery of the union of Christ to the church. A concrete and existential salvific foundation for marriage is built on the archetype of Christ and the church. As church relates to Christ, so couples should relate to each other.

This new theological approach has only been partially translated into new ritual expressions and pastoral outlook. The juridical tone in the formulas and in the priestly function remains central. Unlike many other instances of the Vatican reform, this one represents a compromise between the canonical developments of the marriage institution of the late Middle Ages and the developing personal perspectives of marriage. The classic Roman canonical consent takes the central place, making the Pauline theological inspiration of the covenant of secondary importance. In fact, the rite represents a compromise apparent in the two poles of the rite: the rite of consent of the spouses at the beginning, and the formal blessing toward the end by the priest. It is evidently a duplication of the formal moment of marriage.[52]

One of the main goals of the Vatican II reform was to go back to the biblical theme of marriage. In addition to the above quoted constitutions, the new rite makes this possible with a variety of biblical readings. The reference to biblical themes is one of the major strengths, which offers the possibility of a broad theological reflection to meet the challenges of this floundering institution within a biblical perspective.

Any understanding of the nuptial mystery should stem from the paschal and "anamnestic" reality, since it is from this source that "all the sacraments receive their power."[53] Therefore the links between eucharist and marriage, and baptism and marriage, should be stressed. A united conception of this fundamental sacramentality is found in the power of the mystery of Christ. In the biblical perspective, he transforms all human experience through the indwelling of the sanctifying Spirit. The church invokes the presence and power of the Spirit (*epiclesis*) because the Holy Spirit makes the link between the celebration of God's saving grace and the gift of human love an actual reality. A new domestic church, which is the family, is founded through the covenant of love in the transforming power of the Spirit. Thus the new household becomes a paradigm of friendship, healed and strengthened in a new identity by the presence of the Spirit in the Risen Lord. Furthermore, marriage becomes the incarnate sign of a present covenant. Unfortunately, the *epiclesis* component mentioned above is missing in the 1969 rite of marriage. Contrary to what happens in the eastern liturgies, the specific function of a priest would appear better defined with the more explicit pneumatic dimension.

The Vatican II documents represent a great hope for the future because of their new theological synthesis of conjugal and family life. The actual reform does not go beyond a compromise between the medieval canonical theory of the sacramentality of marriage and the new sacramental theology centered in the neotestamentarian perspective of the salvific mystery. The new liturgy is a hope for the future, since the council encouraged national adaptations and creativity.

### Faith and Sacrament

The most important lesson that can be learned from history, and the only constant essential to this specific tradition, is that marriage "must be in the Lord." This Pauline mandate has been interpreted in two ways: as pastoral care of the church for the couples, and as responsible attitude of Christian couples experiencing their love and commitment to the Lord. The rest, that is, the culturally bound aspect of the sacrament, is secondary: it has been accommodated in the past and can be accommodated in the future.

The values of the society of Paul's time are not far away from those of our Christian world after Christendom. "The end of marriage" of David Morris[54] was unrealistic and naive, but the radical shift of the last decades has stripped marriage and family institutions of the traditional functions of support and proper credibility. The institution, as a small society, shares in the ambiguities and crises of the "great society." Marriage also belongs to the autonomous secular governments and is enmeshed in the prevailing secularist philosophies of the post-Industrial society.

Yet the current pastoral practice still stems from a traditional society of Christendom, where the historical unitarian order of church and state built together the City of God. That order, exemplified by the high Middle Ages, disappeared after the Enlightenment period. The exclusive ecclesiastical marriage was born at a time when the church held a privileged leverage over society.

Today's church is in a mission condition. More than ever, if marriage is to survive, "Christians are told by the Spirit to look to faith" (Gal 5:6). This looking into faith is especially important in regard to "baptized unbelievers" who demand a religious marriage. In our modern pluralistic society, the Pauline mandate to "marry in the Lord" has to prevail over the more sociological concept of "marriage in the church." There has been and will still be a perennial problem. A realistic approach should consider the catechumenal itinerary within the pastoral concern of marriage.

Three different steps of faith, each implying a different degree of involvement with the church, have been identified: (1) a negative or ambiguous attitude of the unchurched person who rejects any dialogue on faith; (2) a religiosity of merely social convenience without a reference to Christ or to personal involvement; and (3) a living Christian faith which is personal and actual. It is possible that these three steps of faith indicate three different stages of sacramentality.

Sacraments presuppose and manifest faith. They also nurture and strengthen it. The new rite is very explicit: seen within a contractual perspective, which emphasizes exchange of rights and duties, these different stages of faith do not pose any problem. But, since Christian marriage is essentially a sign of the covenant of grace between Christ and his church actualized in the human love of a couple, the intention and vision of faith are essential.[55] In that respect J. Wicks rightly states: "that contract can be broken, but covenants are not broken by anyone." Says he, "Today not a few apparently Christian marriages are in fact the union of 'baptized unbelievers' and should not be treated as covenants in the Lord."[56]

Since the demand for a celebration of a natural but transcendent reality totally unsupported by faith is an apparent contraction, priests perhaps need to be reminded that they are "ministers of the Gospel of Christ for all."[57] This tension will always be present in a missionary church. Marriage is a basic sacrament, or a natural sacrament, and, if human love is to be redeemed, it has to be Christ-centered. The truthfulness of the sacrament demands an approach that goes beyond legalities. Lack of readiness for life-long commitment is a serious problem for Christian marriage today.

*Facing New Challenges*

No other area of social life has ever been so subjected to change as has the institution of marriage. Marriage, an act of freedom between two people, has always been strongly conditioned by the multiple factors of the culture of each generation. It is essentially historical; and never before in history has society ever been so subjected to cultural and scientific challenges as the society of today. Consequently, marriage as a culturally conditioned aspect of society is undergoing the profound crisis and the ambiguous trends of our own society.

In past centuries the effort of the church to understand the meaning of marriage was confined to the work of lawyers in the church, but there is an enormous task ahead. Scripture and tradition are essential foundations against which to judge the juridical abstraction of the past. Religious experience must be confronted with the data of behavioral sciences in the case of marriage.

The crisis thus goes beyond the merely religious sphere. A loss of the credibility of marriage and a lack of support of its institution can result. Parallel to this phenomenon, alternative models of marriage are juxtaposed in society. The social outlook is in a continuing flux, from culture to culture and region to region. The following generalizations about the religious situation in our society seem valid: (1) marriage as an institution is less credible; (2) there is a tendency to deny the validity of Christian marriage; and (3) the feeling of belonging to the church is seen to be less relevant.[58]

The efforts of the church in confronting these challenges in the last two decades is apparent, but a gap remains between church practice and people's understanding of marriage. The poignant question here is: What does it mean today to celebrate human love in modern world culture?

A return to the pre-ecclesiastical marriage tradition has been proposed.[59] On the one hand, the church would give up to the civil authority the different facets of the marriage contract.[60] The church would then celebrate the specific sacramental and spiritual aspects in the liturgy. In fact, some of the problem seems to originate, as it has already been noted, from the association between contract and sacrament. However, the separation of church and State and their recognition of competencies and mutual cooperation seem to offset some of the conflictive situations of the post-Tridentine period.

Another point of view advocates the acceptance for the "baptized unbelievers" of the validity of civil marriage. The church, according to Vatican II, recognizes the value of the worldly realities and the autonomy of the State.[61] The unique character of faith, according to which in religious matters no one is to be forced to act against his or her own conscience, is also cited. The practice would eliminate the traditional judgment of a non-sacramental marriage as concubinage. It would mean a return to a pre-Tridentine acknowledgment of the validity of secular marriage. In the ancient and medieval church the hierarchy denied the privilege of the blessing and veiling of the liturgical sacrament for lack of readiness or worthiness (concubinage, for instance). The same cases seem to encourage an opposite pastoral practice today.

Although the traditional pastoral practices still seem inadequate for today's needs, the above considerations overlook the difference between medieval and modern social context. Our society is predominantly secular and individualistic, so marriage for many Christians can remain empty of religious meaning. Neither the neutral State, nor the secularist philosophical currents of our time can give Christian support and meaning for marriage. Marriage is fundamentally a human reality that possesses a natural sacramental character, and therefore it must be inserted into the salvific plan and fulfilled in the primordial sacramental reality of Christ and the church.

History shows us that as the church Christianized the veiling of the familiar pagan rites of the wedding (fourth century), so it also Christianized the classic Roman consent, incorporating it into the sacrament and placing it under its canonical authority for pastoral reasons. Those pastoral reasons, which were the key to the reforms, made the consent of a couple an integral element of the sacrament. Nevertheless, in the final analysis, the ultimate task will always be to reassess the sacramental theory and the pastoral practice against the biblical focus of the covenant. The existential needs of people in today's society and culture must be met, while they remain faithful to the traditional biblical values. In this sense the revised Code represents a step toward balance. Yet it remains only a compromise in the integration of the contribution of the behavioral sciences into the traditional Catholic framework.[62]

Although marriage is in part correctly viewed as a contract, the paramount Christian perspective should view this sacrament as the covenant of the liberating love of the Lord. The biblical covenant, as archetype of the marital union, provides the foundation for the pastoral implementation of an ethical demand beyond the law. The view of marriage as a liberating love-covenant is also the key to reinterpreting the tradition regarding divorce. There were different pastoral practices of the church regarding divorce before the ninth century. Both eastern and western traditions included, before the Carolingian reform, the classic clauses of the Gospel of Matthew on adultery (Mt 5:32; 19:9).[63] Since then the western church has abandoned the broad discipline which would possibly allow divorce, linking itself instead to the doctrine of St. Augustine and St. Jerome, which supported the strict indissolubility of marriage.[64]

Practical solutions to complex situations regarding broken marriages can be quite varied. Specialists in the field have suggested pastoral decisions that correspond to the three levels of sacramentality in marriage: civil marriage (negative attitude on faith), simple religious blessing (mere religiosity), and sacrament (living faith).[65] This pastoral practice would make adaptations in accord with the different degrees of faith operative in the individual marriage and in light of today's pluralistic society.

One of the most original approaches to this complex problem was initiated in the Diocese of Autun, France, at Easter of 1973.[66] This pastoral experiment viewed marriage in three different stages: civil marriage; welcome civil marriage, in which the couple receives a simple blessing in the church after a time of prayer; and the traditional sacramental marriage. Any of these forms implies for the couple a commitment of reflection in faith toward a possible sacramental celebration and the acceptance of the indissolubility of marriage. The goal is the truthfulness of the celebration of an actually covenanted love versus empty formulas aimed at securing merely canonical validity.

*  *  *  *  *  *  *  *  *  *

It is evident that historical theology is a key to interpret the tradition of marriage regarding its anthropological and sacramental reality, ritual creativity, and pastoral alternatives of marriage and remarriage. It provides, therefore, a critical perspective in rethinking the always unfinished integration of the human values of the love-covenant into the paschal mystery. Through the plurality of socio-cultural situations of twenty centuries of experience, historical theology offers models of creativity today and the substantiation of the principle that "sacraments—in this case marriage—exist for people."

*Notes*

1. See David Morris, *The End of Marriage* (London: Cassel, 1971). This book reflects the hypothesis of a future society without the traditional family unit.
2. The doctrinal background of the new canons relies especially on *Gaudium et Spes* 48.
3. Among the best recent books on the historical and theological tradition are: T. Mackin, *What Is Marriage?: Marriage in the Catholic Church* (Ramsey, NJ: Paulist Press, 1982), and W. Kasper, *Theology of Christian Marriage* (New York: The Seabury Press, 1980).
4. O. Rousseau, "Divorce and Remarriage: East and West," *Concilium* 24 (1967) 113 (American edition).
5. Epistle to Diognetus 5:6 (ed. H.I. Marrow, *Sources chrétiennes* 33, 62-63).
6. Canon 54, (J.D. Mansi, *Sacrorum Conciliorum* pt. 2.14).
7. 1 Cor 7:39.
8. *De Corona* 13.4; 14.2 (*Corpus Scriptorum Ecclesiasticorum Latinorum* 70, 182).
9. Letter to Polycarp 5.2 (*Sources chrétiennes* 139).

10. *Stromata* 4.20 (PG 8:1338).

11. G. Martinez, "Graeco-Roman Cultural Symbols and Ritual Creativity Today: An Approach to Marriage," *Questions liturgiques* 65 (1984) 39-52.

12. The most recent research article is R. Béraudy, "Le mariage des chrétiens," *Nouvelle revue théologique* 104 (1982) 50-69. The best study from the perspective of historical theology is still E. Schillebeeckx, *Marriage: Human Reality and Saving Mystery* (New York: Sheed and Ward, 1965).

13. G. Dumézil has published excellent research on marriage in the Greco-Roman world and its Indo-European cultural roots (*Mariages indo-européens, suivi de questions romaines* [Paris: Presses Universitaires de France, 1979] 95-118).

14. See K. Ritzer, *Le Mariage dans les églises chrétiennes: du Ier au XIe siècle* (Paris: Editions du Cerf, 1970) 63.

15. Thus the bishops will oppose the marriage of a Christian woman to a pagan, which meant in practice an apostasy. Tertullian interpreted the words of Paul "marry in the Lord" (1 Cor 7:39) as a mandate to marry a baptized partner (this is the topic of his book *Ad Uxorem*, 2, c.8:6-9 (ed. A. Kroymann, *Corpus Scriptorum Selectorum Latinorum* 1, 393).

16. The *arrha*, or pledge, is first referred to by Tertullian in *Apologeticum* 6.4-6 (PL 1:302-304); thus the wife was *subharrata* (engaged). Regarding the kiss (*osculum*), see *Decrees of Constantine, Codex Theodos*, ed. Haenel, 3.5,6. St. Ambrose wrote in this regard: "Osculum quasi pignus est nuptiarum et praerogativa coniugii" (Epistola 41.18, quoted by M. Righetti in his *Manuale di Storia Liturgica*, vol. 4, 335).

17. From this "veiling of the head" originated the specific term and the Roman rite of marriage (*velatio nuptialis*, see *Sacramentarium Veronense*, no. 1105ff, ed. L.C. Mohlberg, Rerum Ecclesiasticarum Documenta 1 [Rome: Casa Editrice Herder, 1956]). In the east the specific term and rite was *stephanoun*, the nuptial crowning.

18. *Digesta* 35.1, 15. St. Ambrose, who offered a profound theology of marriage in his treatise on virginity, writes: "Non defloratio virginitatis facit coniugium sed pactio coniugalis" (De Inst. Virg. I.6.41 [PL 16:316]).

19. Ritzer, *Le Mariage* 73-79.

20. Edited by F. Brandelione, *Saggi sulla teoria della celebrazione del matrimonio in Italia* (Milan: 1906) 11, note 2.

21. This ancient Roman axiom stresses again the fundamental idea that marriage constitutes the religious and living community of households (*Digesta* 23.2; *Codex Justiniani* 9.32.4).

22. Schillebeeckx, *Marriage* 234.

23. Christian creativity developed a sound integration between the local traditions of the broader Greco-Roman culture and Christian beliefs and ritual expressions. A specific case is the Christian reinterpretation of the meaning of the nuptial veiling and crowning: John Chrysostom will later see in the garland a profound mystical significance (*Homilia 9, in Tim.* [PG 62:546]). For a broader insight of the problem, see A.J. Chupungco, "Greco-Roman Culture and Liturgical Adaptation," *Notitiae* 53 (1979) 208-210.

24. "Unde (vero) sufficiamus ad enarrandam felicitatem eius matrimonii quod ecclesia conciliat, et confirmat oblatio et obsignat benedictio, angeli renuntiant, pater rato habet? Nam nec in terris filii sine consensu patrum rite et iure nubunt." Quoted above, note 15.

25. W.P. Le Saint is right when he affirms that "the passage is one of the most valuable in early Christian literature on the sacred nature of marriage," but his translation is inaccurate, as he sees in it "The Church's role in its celebration" (*Treatises on Marriage and Remarriage: To His Wife* [Westminster, MD: The Newman Press, 1951] 132ff., 142-146).

26. *Sacramentarium Veronense* nos. 1105-110, pp. 139-140.

27. Abrosiaster, *Comm. in Epis. I ad Tim.* 3.12-13 (PL 17:497).

28. *Carmen 25* (*Corpus Scriptorum Ecclesiasticorum Latinorum* 30, 238-245).

29. *Praedestinatus* 3.31 (PL 53:670).

30. *Sermo* 332.4 (PL 38:1463). See Ritzer, *La Mariage* 78-79.

31. Ch. Munier, *Les Statuta Ecclesiae Antiqua* (Paris: 1960) 209-242.

32. *Benedictional of Robert*, ed. W. Greenwell, Publications of Surtees Society 27 (Durham, 1853) 125-132ff.

33. *Rituale Ecclesiae Dunelmensis*, ed. J. Stevenson, Publications of Surtees Society 10 (Durham, 1840) 106-111; see Ritzer, *Le Mariage* 310-318.

34. *Sacramentarium Fuldense S.X.*, ed. G. Richter and A. Schönfelder (Fulda, 1912) nos 2605-2617.

35. *Homilia 9 in Tim* (PG 62:546).

36. *Epistola 321* (PG 37:874).

37. See Ritzer, *La Mariage* 135ff.

38. *Novelle 74*, J. Zepos and P. Zepos, *Ius Graeco-Romanum*, vol. 1 (Athens, 1931) 144-145.

39. Bibliotheca Photii (PG 103:1261).

40. An update of the most important research on the problem based on patristic sources is given by Kasper, *Theology*, footnote 3, pp. 54-57.

41. *Epistola ad Consulta Bulgarorum*, c.3 (PL 119:979): "per hoc sufficiat solus eorum consensus de quorum coniunctione agitur."

42. Research by Ritzer, *Le Mariage* 340-354. These forged writings were incorporated into the *Decretum Gratiani*, the Canon Law of the High Middle Ages.

43. A main source of the rituals of this period is E. Martène, *De Antiquis Ecclesiae Ritibus* (Venice 1788), vol. 2, 120-144; see R. Béraudy, "Le mariage" 67.

44. See the recent study done by T. Mackin, *What Is Marriage?* 161-164 and 192-199.

45. "Manifestatio consensus nuptialis per verba de praesenti in facie ecclesiae," according to the teachings of the twelfth-century theologians and of early scholasticism. See for this period of history the important research of J.B. Molin and P. Mutembe, *Le Rituel du mariage en France du XIIe au XVIe siècle* (Paris: Beauchesne, 1973) 283-318.

46. What is the sign that actually confers grace and founds the sacramental bond? What is the essence of marriage? Are the spouses themselves ministers of the sacrament? Does their mutual consent found marriage, or is the priest the proper minister through the prayer of blessing? These are some of the main questions addressed by the scholastic theologians.

47. *De Nuptiis et Concupiscentia* I.11 (PL 44:420); *De Bono Coniugali* 32 (PL 40:394); *Contra Julianum* 3.57 (PL 44:732), among others.

48. Following the line of indissolubility, the objective sacramental character was defined, such as the Council of Lyons did in 1274: "It is clear, then," argues W. Kasper, "that the Council of Trent taught unambiguously the indissolubility of marriage, but that it did not intend to summarize or systematize the whole of the Church's tradition or to provide an all-embracing doctrine of the indissolubility of marriage" (*Theology* 62).

49. *Le Sacramentaire grégorien*, ed. J. Deshusses, Specilegium Friburgense 16 (Fribourg: Editions Universitaires Frigourg Suisse, 1971) no. 838a: "Deus qui tam excellenti mysterio coniugalem copulam consecrasti, ut Christi et ecclesiae sacramentum praesignares in foedere nuptiarum."

50. The important canon 7 defines the indissolubility of marriage and presents the sacrament as a matter of the church, but avoided any condemnation of the past tradition of the early Fathers and the Eastern Church regarding flexibility in the case of divorce and remarriage.

51. Particularly *Sacrosanctum Concilium* 77-78; *Lumen Gentium* 41; *Gaudium et Spes* 47-53.

52. See the excellent study of P.-M. Gy, "Le nouveau ritual romain du mariage," *La Maison-Dieu* 99 (1969) 136.

53. *Sacrosanctum Concilium* 61.

54. Morris, *The End of Marriage*.

55. The Rite of Marriage (1990), Introduction nos. 7-9.

56. J. Wicks, "Marriage: An Historical and Theological Overview," in M.J. Taylor and others, *The Sacraments* (New York: Alba House, 1981) 190.

57. The Rite of Marriage (1990), Introduction no. 9.

58. Although the problem is much more complex, and attitudes vary with cultural trends, essential similarities seem predominant in Western Europe and the United States. See "The Apostolic Exhortation on the Family" (1980 Synod of Bishops) nos. 6-11, in *Origins* 11 (1981) 440-441; also Philippe Beguérie, "Problèmes actuels dans la pastoral du mariage en France," *La Maison-Dieu* 127 (1976) 8-9.

59. This tradition (before the ninth century) was common to the east and west in its parallel ritual features and theological content, namely, the flexible pastoral attitude of evangelical compassion toward re-married Christians. Such an evangelical story of compassion in the light of the covenant was overlooked when the ethical imperative of the covenanted love became for the canonist an absolute code of indissolubility, and when the scholastics of the twelfth century applied to marriage the verticalism of the transcendent efficacy of the sacraments.

60. This is the case, for instance, of the Chaldean rite today which does not include mutual consent; see Kl. Richter, "The Liturgical Celebration of Marriage: The Problems Raised by Changing Theological and Legal Views of Marriage," *Concilium* 87 (1973) 72-87 (American edition).

61. *Gaudium et Spes* 36, 74; *Dignitatis Humanae* 2, 3, 10.

62. See J.A. Alessandro, "Marriage and the Revised Code," *New Catholic World* 226 (1983) 126-131.

63. Even the Council of Trent showed moderation in this regard, as stated above. Tridentine theologians, such as Cajetan and Ambrosius Catharinus, reaffirmed the old tradition of leniency in regard to the quoted Matthaean clauses. Says E. Schillebeeckx, "The Church did not in this canon 7 (decree *Tametsi*) solemnly define in a direct manner the indissolubility of Christian marriage in the case of adultery" (*Marriage*, note 2).

64. P. Nautin, "Divorce et remariage dans la tradition de l'église latine," *Recherches de science religieuse* 62 (1974) 54.

65. J.A. Schmeiser, "Marriage: New Alternatives," *Worship* 55 (1981) 26.

66. A complete account of the Autun pastoral project is given by J.A. Schmeiser, ibid., 23-34.

# 4

## Marriage as Sacramental Mystery: A Sign of Love

IN ORDER TO MEET THE PRESENT CRISIS OF MARRIAGE, THEOLOGIANS must acquire a deeper understanding of its sacramentality by laying bare the anthropological and theological roots which constitute its essential dimensions. A Christian marriage is not only a partnership, but a grace-filled relationship whose essence is love. This relationship establishes, on the one hand, an intimate bond between two people and, on the other, the symbolic expression of something higher and transcendental. To understand the sacramentality of marriage we have to go deeper into the complex meaning of a human relationship, considered not in the abstract, but as a liberating and salvific experience lived in the historical reality of today's society.

In fact, as cultural anthropology demonstrates, the institution of marriage has always been a human and historical reality actualized by a free act in a variety of forms. The sacramental experience of a person, though always rooted in the same Christian mystery, is nevertheless understood within the context of mutable human perceptions and needs. An appreciation of the sacramentality of marriage demands, accordingly, a renewed vision of its interpersonal and social, ecclesial and canonical, ritual and spiritual aspects. However, theology has to

focus primarily on the interpersonal and ecclesial aspects because sacraments interpret the existential and personal reality
in which the mystery is embedded. Therefore, in the case of
marriage, the mystery can only transform that reality when
the sacramental vision actually bears some relation to the basic
experience of married people. What is of vital importance is
not only the relationship between faith and sacramentality,
but the connection between the meaning of marriage as a sacrament and the reality of the Christian couple within our secular society. Walter Kasper comments that "it is very disturbing
that there is hardly any other sphere of human life today in
which the discrepancy between the official teaching of the
church and the convictions and practice of very many Christians is so great as in questions of sexuality and marriage."[1]

Perfunctory rituals that are, apparently, automatically sacramental might have a valid social and canonical function, but
they are not equivalent to a sacramental and spiritual event
rooted by faith in the Christological mystery. However, despite the explicit lack of faith, there is a religious celebration,
and even a certain human sacramentality, whenever the nuptial solemnization is authentically rooted in the symbolism of
love. That is why the interpersonal and ecclesial aspects are
the two hinges of Christian sacramentality. The real challenge
will always be to make the whole sacramental event credible
and meaningful in human and biblical terms.

We shall explore, first, the theological tradition and, second,
the meaning of sacramentality in order to validate the thesis of
this chapter: the fundamental and life-long sacramental meaning of all dimensions of conjugal life is the expression of baptismal sacramentality.

## THE THEOLOGICAL TRADITION

The different aspects explain, on the one hand, the multiplicity of historical forms marriage has assumed and, on the
other, the equally complex and perplexing evolution of the
idea of sacramentality. This evolutional process of secular
marriage into ecclesiastical marriage can be divided into two
periods corresponding, in general, to the two millennia of
Christianity. Marriage was officially recognized as one of the

seven sacraments first by Peter Lombard in the twelfth century, although not without hesitation on how and why it was a sacrament.

### From Mystery to Sacrament

The secular character of marriage in the patristic period does not imply in the least that marriage was profane and unholy.[2] On the contrary, marriage like the whole of life was considered sacred by the Greco-Roman religious world-view and by the Christian faith. Secular here refers to the lack of any Christian sacralization of the institution, juridical language, or ritual efficacy in the Christian praxis of marriage. This praxis is equidistant between the sacral and profane orders because the marriage of a baptized person is centered at the heart of the mystery of Christ. This incorporation into Christ founded the Christian matrix of a marital union which the praxis of the patristic church saw exclusively from a biblical and ecclesial focus.

A more concrete approach to the evolution of the study of sacramentality has to consider the three major perspectives of the marriage institution: juridical, anthropological, and theological. The first two perspectives, which deal respectively with a contract and a relationship, indirectly clarify the third and major perspective, the sacramental. From a social and legal standpoint, Christians celebrate their marriage like non-Christians since they adopt the cultural symbolism of their society, with its traditions and Roman law.

The religious understanding of marriage held by Christians, however, was exclusively rooted in biblical tradition, as various "commentaries" demonstrate.[3] A gradual process of many centuries of inculturation imbued the Roman celebrative elements (symbolism, customs, and law) with the meaning of the covenant and the Christian moral code. The veiling of the bride in fourth-century Rome and the crowning of the couple in the eastern provinces are the best examples of this process of inculturation. They were two constitutive rites in early Christianity and important sources of sacramental theology.[4]

The way early writers understood interpersonal and sexual relations in conjugal life reflected a negative view of sexuality, a suspicion of the body typical of the time, and their acceptance of woman's inferior social status. No doubt this ambivalence toward the body was an obstacle not only because it kept them from seeing the body as a sacramental symbol (as we might today), but also because it was "an important cultural obstacle to the full acknowledgement of the sacramentality of Marriage."[5]

It was not yet culturally possible to integrate the intersubjective and human values completely into the saving mystery. The anthropological impasse which conditioned their ethical and spiritual understanding of marriage, did not prevent the Fathers of the Church from seeing marriage, elevated by grace, as a salvific sign founded on the reality of creation and an actual symbol of the mystery of Christ's love for the church. Their sacramental theology draws insight from this paradigmatic biblical view.

Christ did not institute marriage at any concrete moment of his life or by any particular mandate, but by his whole ministry which culminated in his own passover. From this horizon of faith, which comprehends all of Christ's redemptive life and teaching, the Fathers developed the Christological and ecclesial meaning of the conjugal union of spouses. It would be anachronistic to see in patristic terminology the technical category of a specific sacrament. The words they used—mystery, image, and type—have a deeper, broader, and analogical meaning. The reality of marriage was a revelatory and participatory sign of the liberating love of Christ for the church. The spouses have a vital share in the mystery which their union symbolizes. The Second Letter of Clement (circa A.D. 150) speaks in these terms from the Christ-church perspective although, in this particular case, it praises the celibate relationship of the spouses.[6]

Early church literature has no treatise on marriage (except Tertullian's "To His Wife"), although many references to marriage are found in the Fathers' writings on virginity. Genesis and the Letter to the Ephesians were two major inspirations for their theology of marriage.[7]

In their comments on these key passages, the Fathers insist that the human and created reality of marriage is not only the present realization of the creativity of God, but also a particular mode of being of the Christ-church mystery. For Tertullian, conjugal union is an image and symbol of the divine covenant: "If you accept Christ and the church, you must also accept what is his image, symbol, and sacrament."[8] The early writers wanted to stress the dignity and value of marriage whose pristine created purpose Christ restored; but their vision cannot be reduced to ethical and pastoral considerations. It also has a sacramental dimension stemming from the re-creational and salvific foundation of Christ and the all-embracing and universal mystery of the church. This implies a dynamic conception of Christian existence, and hence of marriage, which is not limited by virtue of an efficacious ritual power or sacramental function, but extends to the whole of the life embraced by Christ. The sacraments of Christian initiation provide the radical spiritual depth and the sacramental foundation of marriage.[9]

This total reality of salvation, already present in the eternal value of the mission of Christ, was the paradigmatic center of patristic sacramental theology from which marriage was understood. There was a progression in general from the *Christus victor* of the earlier writers to the *Christus sanctificator* of later patristic theology (fourth and fifth centuries). A more elaborate theology of the sacraments developed from this perspective. This was also true in regard to marriage which was always seen in intimate relation to baptism and the eucharist. The eucharist, according to Simeon of Thessalonica, "perfects and seals every sacrament and every divine mystery."[10] According to St. Ambrose, through the sanctifying reality of Christ in baptism and the gift of grace, Christian marriage has a new meaning. He sees the first marriage of Adam and Eve as a symbol of the "sacrament" of the Christ-church mystery.[11] His insistence on the ecclesial dimension of marriage, through the blessing of the spouses by the bishop or priest, has a symbolic and broad sacramental meaning.

St. Augustine provides the best and most complete patristic synthesis. He represents a further development in the theology of marriage, despite the negative influence of Hellenistic dualism on his view of sexuality. His major contribution, which influenced medieval thinking and reached modern times, is his characterization of the threefold goods of marriage: offspring, faithfulness, and sacrament. The ecclesial character of marriage, which made the participation of the bishop appropriate, is also a reality. However, it has to be understood in relation to baptism and the eucharist, and cannot be reduced to the sphere of a sacramental function. He understands sacrament in the broad sense of "mystery" which includes both the hidden spiritual reality of the saving action of Christ, and the sacramental actions which introduce Christians into that reality: "What is celebrated visibly . . . is understood vitally in Christ.[12] In this regard, marriage, a good given by God and healed by redemptive grace, is seen as a meaningful sign of the mystery of Christ and his church. The sacramental reality of marriage is the foundation and source of all its other values, including indissolubility, because in Christian marriage "the holiness of the sacrament is more valuable than the fertility of the womb."[13]

The eastern patristic tradition also conceptualizes marriage from the broad level of sacrament as mystery. Origen (third century) and John Chrysostom (fourth century) are among its major theologians. Marriage is understood as a full realization of God's creative purpose which has the capability of effectively signifying the original sacrament of Christ-church. Chrysostom, who calls marriage the "sacrament of love," sees the intimate union of the spouses integrated in the eternal redemptive mission of Christ.[14] In the theology of both the Latin and Greek Fathers, this human realization has an essential correlative in the vocation of virginity. In the east, the human values of marriage were glorified more than in the Latin tradition by the eschatological vision of the new meaning Christ gave marriage and the transformation this wrought. Orthodox Christians certainly reached a theological depth, exuberant symbolic celebration, and pastoral realism from a biblico-liturgical focal point unmatched by other traditions. John Meyendorff rightly states that the Orthodox understanding of "the sacrament of marriage suggests the only possible Christian attitude towards most of the issues raised today."[15]

*From Covenant to Contract*

A paradigmatic shift took place in medieval times (from the eleventh century on) which Henri de Lubac characterized as the passage "from symbol to dialectic."[16] Patristic terminology, culturally rooted in Platonism, was reinterpreted in the more abstract and rational Aristotelian framework. The symbolic language, which pointed beyond itself as a sign-synthesis of an interior reality and transcendent mystery, took the new meaning of an external and sometimes allegorical sign. Within this cultural-religious context, the marriage *in esse*, or the mode of being, of the patristic theology became the marriage *in fieri*, or to be done, of scholastic theology (eleventh and thirteenth centuries) and of the church down through the centuries. The emphasis changed from the mystery signified by the sign to the sacramental character of the sign understood in a narrow sense. The effort to establish the essential element of the sacramental validity of marriage (consent or *copula*) led to the prevalent canonical mentality. The first official declaration of marriage as a sacrament was made in 1184 at the Council of Verona.

The long evolutional process toward a full acknowledgement of marriage as one of the seven sacraments culminated in the more positive synthesis offered by Thomas Aquinas. Within the anthropological limitations of his age, he succeeded in integrating the Augustinian values of marriage by making them the ends of marriage in a new conception of its full sacramental dignity. This dignity stemmed from the presence of grace because in the Thomistic perspective the sacraments of the new covenant provide the grace they signify. In Thomas' conception, the ends of marriage (procreation, faithfulness, and sacrament) provide the total meaning of human sexuality, which he values from the point of view of self-surrender. Thus Christian marriage is like a cultic act, especially from the perspective of the participation of the spouses in the love of Christ for the church. Some ambivalence toward human sexuality remains in this traditional functionalist understanding of marriage as subordinate to the primary end of procreation. As Thomas states in reference to the ends of marriage, "The first end is found in marriage insofar as man is animal, the second insofar as he is man, the third insofar as he is believer."[17] This intelligent Thomistic presentation represents a considerable development in the theology of marriage in doctrinal terms and especially inasmuch as it is a sacramental sign.

From a liturgical and theological point of view, the ecclesiastical marriage which prevailed from the eleventh to the thirteenth centuries and onwards did not represent much progress, especially in relation to the broad Thomistic conception. Under the influence of the two major factors in the evolution of the structures of marriage, namely, new social conditions and the new preoccupations they bring to the magisterium, theological reflection evolved toward a more rationalistic and juridical conception of marriage.

## THE MEANING OF SACRAMENTALITY

Sacraments are signs composed of words and images which religious people use to communicate and celebrate life's meaning in its depth, symbolism, and transcendence. Through a symbolic sacramental action, the basic human experience is transformed in its depth and sanctified by divine goodness. From a Christian perspective, this action has to include the central focus on Christ as the embodiment of God's saving action in history, living in the church which is the fundamental reality of Christ's presence. Sacraments, therefore, become vital signs of the mystery of Christ in people.

How does marriage fit into the symbolic and sacramental context? Marriage is first of all a primary and universal sign. In fact, it is a sign with complex meanings and levels of reality. It is a sign of a dense anthropological and social reality, which refers to the total experience of a man and a woman and the communication between them. Interchange, donation, communication, and intimate sharing are not only essential characteristics of conjugal life but, as a whole, potentially sacramental. However, in order to call this conjugal experience Christian, it has to be seen in the light of the mystery of Christ.

An approach to the sacramentality of marriage can be developed, therefore, from a theology of the sacramental sign. However, this can be understood in two ways. This sign can be understood analytically and juridically, or in terms of its rich biblical and anthropological relevance. The former approach, which is concerned with the valid and effective sacramental sign seen exclusively in the consent expressed by the couple, is the one taken by scholastic theology and canon law. Only the latter approach can provide the fundamental perspective of the transforming significance of a marriage intentionally lived and celebrated "in the Lord."

The concept of sacramental sign is also needed to place marriage in the traditional sevenfold sacramental structure. This concept can be only applied to marriage in relation to other sacraments analogously. From the point of view of the sign and its meaning, marriage is a different sacrament. Its sign is a committed love which is grounded in faith; its meaning is the salvation of a personal community. Marriage, in fact, is a unique sign of a salvific reality through which the couple shares in the mystery of Christ and becomes a new way of being in the church.

From the perspective of the sign, marriage is essentially a sign, not only of life, but of the whole of life. It cannot be reduced to a sacred function or ritual, because it is a sign in all its human fullness and transcendent reality. In acknowledging that all human experience is fundamentally sacramental and is transformed by Christ, Bernard Cooke calls marriage a basic and key sacrament of the saving presence of God to human life. In this regard, marriage in its symbolic and revelatory meaning points to something beyond itself, and is "a paradigm of human relationship and love."[18] This general approach to conjugal sacramentality is confirmed by modern sacramental theology which emphasizes, on the one hand, the reality of a sacrament broadly seen in the context of the sacramental dimensions of all human life and the totality of the person realized by Christ and, on the other, the importance of stressing the sacramental dimension of Christianity as one of its original and essential characteristics.

This wider vision has to find its roots in biblical revelation and patristic theology which constitute the real foundation of the Christian tradition of marriage. Although the patristic and liturgical conception of the sacramental mystery ceased to be the major focus in the theology of marriage after scholasticism, that tradition reached the twelfth century, in which a real pluralism in the understanding of the nature of the sacrament and marital love still existed[19] and it remained alive in the liturgical formularies of the Western and Eastern Churches.

The patristic-liturgical tradition certainly needs to be reinterpreted in the light of a modern biblical and personalist anthropology, but nonetheless, it provides major perspectives
which represent an essential link with the New Testament
sources of the sacraments. These major perspectives are the
following: (1) an understanding of marriage in the historic-
salvific perspective of the covenant realized in Christ; (2) the
Christocentric foundation of the sacramental dignity of a
Christian marriage; (3) and the acknowledgement that this
personal bond remains perennially salvific within the sphere
of Christ, that is, "according to the spirit," and as a true "spiritual generation."[20] The Fathers looked at the concrete and existential aspects of the human partnership which is based in
the order of creation, but whose ultimate meaning was restored and elevated by Christ. From their approach to the biblical symbolism of various texts, especially Ephesians 5, they
developed their understanding of the sacramental reality
which referred to the totality of life and extended to the
whole length of the conjugal relationship. This life is sacramental in its own right within the all-embracing sacramental
mystery of the church.

The above introductory framework is based on a historic-
salvific and personalist perspective of marriage as a sign of the
paschal mystery of Christ in a double sense: (1) in its sacramental symbolism, as a prophetic sign of the mystery of
Christ, and (2) in its sacramental mystery, as an actual sharing
in the saving mission of Christ. As Vatican II states in regard
to the sacrament, "the spouses signify and share the mystery
of the unity and faithful love between Christ and the
Church."[21] This living sacramentality depends, consequently,
on two essential and inseparable dimensions: the anthropological (marriage is an effective sign) and the theological (God's
saving love is made present).

### Sacramental Symbolism

If the reality of marriage is rooted in its symbolic meaning,
the Christian realization of its symbolic meaning is rooted in
the actualization of the mystery of Christ. Such is the perspective of Paul (Eph 5:32) who, inspired by the nuptial symbolism

of the covenant, uses "the language of sacramental sign-value."[22] The understanding of marriage sacramentality flows from this relationship. On the one hand, the complex symbolic meanings of marriage, like intimate love, should be valued as personally and effectively real, and as the way to know its nature and touch its mystery. On the other hand, these complex symbolic meanings, which are the way of being of the conjugal partnership, have to be celebrated in the sacramental accomplishment of the mystery and lived out "in the Lord." The former represents human marriage, which is a powerful symbol in itself; the latter, which includes faith, refers to the Christian sacrament. In more concrete terms, love is the symbol of marriage because love is not only the action of marriage but, above all, the heart of its meaning and reality. Because a sacrament is a symbolic action, the fundamental reality of love provides the matter of marriage's sacramental symbolism. Marriage is, in fact, the sacrament of love.[23]

In the past, this symbolic perspective was not sufficiently appreciated for at least two reasons which are related to one another: the predominantly theoretical and rational approach to marriage in preconciliar theology, and the indigence of symbolic imagination in modern culture. Marriage is profound because it is an intimate partnership. It is only here that we can find its religious roots[24] by considering its anthropological and biblical relevance. On the one hand, by investing the sexuality, personal encounter, sacrificial love, and permanent faithfulness of marriage with full symbolic meaning, the potentiality of its sacramentality is already seen. Nevertheless, the core of that symbolism and sacramental reality does not emerge meaningfully when marriage is reduced to the simple sacralization of a social contract. On the other hand, the symbolic deficit of our present pragmatic and rationalistic culture inhibits the development of the sense of mystery, gratuity, and the symbolic dimensions of human existence. In fact, movement toward commitment in marriage is a dynamic progression through stages involving a life-creating mystery which fosters the self-disclosure and freedom characteristic of a successful conjugal relationship. Ultimately, the mystery of the intimate relationship of marital life draws its full meaning and grace from Christ, the fullness of the mystery of God, "in whom the love of God toward humankind has been revealed" (Ti 2:11).

This symbolic perspective integrates the natural and the supernatural, the personal and biblical aspects, so that conjugal communion is seen as "an anthropological synthesis between grace and life."[25] Marriage needs, in fact, to have the different aspects of its reality: human and divine, creative and redemptive, personal and social, existential and ecclesial harmoniously integrated in the sacramental sign. All these aspects have to enter into a theological reflection seen against the background of the socio-cultural evolution of the institution and grounded in the primordial sacramental sign of God's grace and fidelity, Christ, who bound himself to history. From this perspective the sacramental sign-value of marriage is all-embracing and life-long.

Marriage is an all-embracing symbol and reality because of the centrality of love, which makes marriage a paradigm of an interpersonal relationship. This intimate partnership establishes the couple in a mutual, faithful, fruitful, permanent, and public union. In embracing all the natural values and facets of this partnership, the sacramental sign signifies and realizes the harmony between life and grace, the natural and the supernatural. Love and sexuality, procreation and caring, intimacy and communication, and all the hopes and struggles of the intimate and familial lives of the spouses are not just natural phenomenon, but salvific mystery. Their union is sacramental at its core as a privileged encounter of the divine whenever their relationship is lived authentically in faith.

The marriage symbolism also reveals the permanent and dynamic reality of the conjugal communion. Vatican II states this permanent and living sacramental reality from the perspective of biblical symbolism, and speaks about a quasi-consecration of this communion by the presence of Christ in the life of the spouses.[26] This life-long sacramental reality cannot be adequately explained from the point of view of a contractual commitment and sexual consummation. In the past this view led to the idea of marriage as a static reality and institution, initiated by the completion of a human and religious development. Before and after the wedding the dynamic nature of marriage, seen in both its human reality and in the perspective of the covenant, indicates a gradual and progressive journey of many stages. Like the biblical covenant in its actualization in the church, the marriage journey is already realized, and yet always in need of growth. This perspective of a lifetime sacramental journey is pregnant with important implications for the pastoral and theological understanding of the sacramentality of marriage.[27] A personalist theology provides the key to Christian marriage: "the bond is made for the person." This focus stems, in fact, from the perspective of a sacramental man-woman relationship founded on the baptismal consecration, celebrated in the ecclesial community, and perfected in a life-long bond of communion.

In conclusion, the essence of marriage as a permanent sacrament cannot be explained by the force of consent (a juridical category), but only by the love relationship itself (personalist view) because "this relationship is the sacrament first and foremost and in its own right."[28]

### Sacramental Mystery

The sacramental mystery of marriage is anchored in its human reality open to transcendence. It is this which makes marriage a radically human sacrament. Friendship, passion and uncontrolled love, body and spirit, intimacy and communication, respect and forgiveness, self-control and responsibility, and the total reality of a committed partnership, are part of the sacramental experience of the couple. These elements are not unique to Christians, but Christians do live them in a new way because of God's liberating love poured forth in Christ. This total reality, especially the centrality of conjugal love, constitutes the human foundation of marriage as a sacrament. When two Christians marry, God is present within their human partnership which has been subsumed by the redeeming force of Christ who is part of creation and head of it (Col 1:16). David Thomas expands the sacramental meaning and experience to five different and related levels (dimensions) of Christian marriage: the sexual, the creative, the loving, the ecclesial, and the spiritual. They are organically related and mutually interdependent. "Christian marriage is, therefore, a genuine sign/symbol/sacrament that God's presence, love, and power are present in the real world, and that the married can, if willing, make God quite real in bed, board, babies, and backyard."[29]

The human and divine realities are present in marriage not only because all creation is potentially sacramental, but because marriage signifies and makes mystery present. It is, in fact, as Walter Kasper sees it from a biblical perspective, "the grammar that God uses to express his love and faithfulness."[30] In this regard marriage is, in itself, a natural sacrament, that is, a radical hope of salvation and an actual means to it. In fact, marriage is a sacrament not because it is a sign of Christ's love for his church. It is a sign of Christ's love for his church because it is, in itself, a sacrament; that is, a natural sign of salvific actualization and self-transcendency which can express the core of the Christian mystery.

St. Augustine acknowledges that the marriage of non-Christians is a "sacrament-bond" of a sacred and mysterious reality, which nevertheless calls for the fullness and self-revelation of the Christian mystery.[31] This acknowledgement of different degrees of sacramentality is an important key to the theology of marriage sacramentality. There are three degrees: marriage is a *natural sacrament* in its own right instituted by God, a *covenant sacrament* as a prophetic symbol of the community of grace and salvation between Yahweh and Israel and, finally, a *Christian sacrament* as revealed by Jesus in terms of humanity's new being in the salvific order of redemption. God's self-gift, which is symbolized and realized at the heart of every authentic human partnership, Christian or non-Christian, calls upon people to acknowledge, celebrate, and live that humanly fragile partnership as a sign and reality of Christ's saving grace and fidelity.

What, then, is the full meaning and unique reality of Christian marriage? What makes this natural sacrament a specifically Christian sacrament? Once more the key to the sacramental reality is not in the act of marrying itself, but before it, specifically in the Jesus-relationship of the baptismal consecration which incorporates a Christian into the Body of Christ. The sacraments of Christian initiation (baptism of the Spirit and eucharist) are the true foundation of marriage because through faith the baptized person participates in the divine self-giving by means of the sanctifying presence of Christ. It is this newness in and through the relationship with Christ which makes the couple a new being in the church. This new being of the Christian couple is, in fact, in the words of Karl Rahner, "the very fulfillment of the Church."[32] The formal marriage covenant makes the reality of that new being explicit in the partnership of two people who surrender to Christ's abiding presence in their self-gift to each other.

This baptismal vocation is the sacramental foundation of marriage which makes the union of two Christians different from the natural contract of marriage. Both unions, Christian and non-Christian, share the same anthropological, socio-cultural, and religious reality. Furthermore, both unions are signs of the mystery of God and Christ and, when authentically lived, are spiritually fruitful because God's grace is not indifferent to the human love he created.[33] However, only Christian marriage is "in Christ." The new being in Christ is the essence of Christian sacramentality called to live the salvific Christ-church mystery in loyalty, service, and obedience. Christ is the ultimate potential for the spouses to actually be "grace" to one another because they are "guided and enriched by the redeeming power of Christ and the Church's mediation of salvation."[34]

The specific elements of Christian marriage stem from this Christ-church-spouses relationship. Consequently, faith, baptism, and community respectively constitute the personal, ontological, and ecclesial qualifications of the Christian sacramentality of marriage.[35] Baptism is the foundation on which the intimate partnership of the spouses is built in the image of Christ and through which it really becomes (ontologically) a "new way of being" in the church. But baptism, like marriage, expresses the faith of an individual incorporated into the Body of Christ. The vital connection between these three qualifications makes the solemnization of the marriage of the baptized non-believer not only empty of sacramental meaning, but also non-Christian.[36]

Marriage is, in fact, a sacrament of faith and not simply a ritual function. It is a life process in which two people interpret and live out their gift and commitment to one another. The symbolic and ritual function is only the high point of the process. Since the symbolic function celebrates the actualization of the total mystery of Christ lived by the baptized in the specific crucial situation of his or her life, it provides the key allowing us to interpret the marriage journey as a grace-full relationship. The human components of marriage constitute the "matter" of the sacrament. Professed faith is the element that makes the difference.[37] Baptized non-believers nevertheless pose a dilemma. On the one hand, a sacrament is a sign and a mystery of faith, a faith which cannot be measured; but, on the other hand, only personal belief can prevent Christian sacramentality. Sacramental truthfulness and the authentic experience of faith depend more on Christian initiation than on marriage itself.

Consequently, although the church should not disregard the canonical and extra-theological prerequisites, its role should be primarily theological and pastoral. This obviously calls for a total ministry to marriage and to the family as the foundational church which takes a predominantly prophetic and spiritual orientation, rather than one that is overly canonical. Needless to say, the personalist orientation includes and presupposes the institutional and contractual aspects, which are, nevertheless, subordinate to the covenantal understanding.

As a new being within the Body of Christ, the baptized makes an option in the church. The sacrament of marriage is not only a public commitment, but a concretization of the universal sacrament of the church. Consequently, its ecclesial reality implies the celebration of the sacramental sign before the community. What is important is not the ritualization in itself. The secular reality of the marriage of the baptized is already holy and sacramental by its nature, that is, it shares in the sphere of God's holiness through Christ's redemptive ministry. We celebrate not to make marriage holy, but because it is holy, and, as sign of faith, it demands a public and ecclesial expression. The need for a symbolic and sacramental celebration does not come from the outside, but from life itself which is sustained by a sharing in the divine source and the redeeming love of Christ.

The couple is called to celebrate in the community what their union represents, the Christ-church nuptial union, and what their union symbolizes, God's self-gift in the sanctifying encounter and presence of Christ. In fact, "the Lord encounters Christian spouses through the sacrament of marriage."[38]

While considering the baptismal character, Scheeben points out that there is a real, essential, and intrinsic relationship between sacramental marriage and the mystery of Christ and the church. Marriage participates actively and effectively in that fundamental mystery.[39]

The need for a sacramental celebration is also obvious when marriage is looked at as a critical religious passage of life and intimacy. As such, it calls for the clarification of meaning in the vision of faith and the acknowledgment of the gift of self. It also makes it possible to integrate the complex values of a partnership through the unconditional love and healing grace of Christ. The sacrament of marriage thus becomes a particular actualization of the baptismal vocation.[40] This is exactly what the ritualization of the sacrament means: the permanent manifestation and actualization (*anamnesis*) of the new covenant of Christ. The sacramental reality remains in the life of the couple who continue to represent the mystery and be a sacrament to one another, to their family, and to the community of faith. They are the actualizing sign of God's love to the world.

* * * * * * * * * *

The essential character of Christian marriage can be cogently understood, both theologically and pastorally, when it is considered in terms of the broad meaning of the sacrament as mystery. This concept was developed here from the perspective of the symbolic reality of the union between the human and the divine seen in the human experience of marital communion. It is a communion which signifies and partakes of Christ's redeeming and never-ending love. This approach makes it possible to correlate the personalist view of an intimate partnership and its interpretation from a Christological and ecclesial basis. Its human reality as a community of caring, forgiveness and service, and as a saving mystery of grace constitutes the full sacramental and spiritual identity of Christian marriage. From the perspectives of human, biblical, and ecclesial symbolism, marriage is seen to be fundamentally a sign-synthesis of life, faith, and love—a mystery of grace.

*Notes*

1. Walter Kasper, *Theology of Christian Marriage* (New York: The Seabury Press, 1980) 1-2. Within the vast bibliography on the sacramentality of marriage, I draw attention to three current studies: Susan Wood, "The Marriage of Baptized Nonbelievers: Faith, Contract, and Sacrament," *Theological Studies* 48 (1987) 279-301; William P. Roberts, ed., *Commitment to Partnership: Explorations of the Theology of Marriage* (New York: Paulist Press, 1987); Roger Béraudy, *Sacrement de mariage: Questions et perspectives* (Paris: Desclée, 1985).

2. "Christians marry according to Roman law," states Arnobius in his *Adversus Nationes*, I.2 (*Corpus Scriptorum Ecclesiasticorum Latinorum* 4, 5); although the pastoral concern of the church is well documented from the very beginning: "Christians "marry in the Lord" (1 Cor 7:39).

3. The spiritual roots of marriage were developed from the biblical sources, especially the sacramental vision of Ephesians 5:22-32; see Aimé-Georges Martimort, "The Contribution of Liturgical History to the Theology of Marriage," in *Contemporary Perspectives on Christian Marriage: Propositions and Papers from the International Theological Commission*, ed. Richard Malone and John R. Connery (Chicago: Loyola University Press, 1984) 297-312.

4. See German Martinez, "Marriage: Historical Developments and Future Alternatives," *The American Benedictine Review* 37 (1986) 376-380.

5. According to Louis-Marie Chauvet in regard to both the patristic and the medieval theologians: see his "Le mariage un sacrement pas comme les autres," *La Maison-Dieu* 127 (1976) 89. St. Jerome says that "the husband who abstains from sexual relations honors his wife, and if he loves with too much passion commits adultery" (*Adversus Jovinianum* I.49 [PL 23:293-294]).

6. Clement of Rome, *Epistola II ad Virgines*, ch. 14-15 (PG 1:444-450).

7. In particular, Gn 1:2, Jn 2:1-11, Mt 5:32, 19:9, and Eph 5:21-33.

8. Tertullian, *De Monogamia* XA.1-2 (PL 2:994).

9. Whereas this patristic terminology should not be understood in terms of the Tridentine meaning of a sacrament, but in a biblico-liturgical context, it certainly provides a rich and multivalent concept of marriage as sacramental mystery; see Christine Mohrmann, "Sacramentum dans les plus anciens textes chrétiens," in her *Etudes sur le latin des chrétiens*, vol. 1 (Rome: Edizioni di Storia e Letteratura, 1958) 233-244. Tertullian provides one of the most explicit examples of the sacramentality of marriage not implying any specific liturgical

rite of marriage; see Martimort "The Contribution" 298; also Martinez, "Marriage" 376-377.

10. Simeon of Thessalonica, *Dialogos*, ch. 282 (PG 155:512). "It is the eucharist which gives to marriage its specifically Christian meaning," according to early Christian writers (John Meyendorff, *Marriage: An Orthodox Perspective* [New York: St. Vladimir's Seminary Press, 1970] 24).

11. Ambrose, *Epistola* 77.4 (PL 16:1270).

12. Augustine, *Sermo* 10.2 (PL 38:93).

13. Augustine, *De Bono Coniungali*, ch. 18.21 (PL 40:388); Maurice Jourjon, *Les Sacrements de la liberté chrétienne selon l'église ancienne* (Paris: Les Editions du Cerf, 1981) 127-141; *Gaudium et Spes* 48.

14. John Chrysostom. *Epistola I ad Cor.* 9.3 (51:230); Henri Crouzel, "Le mariage des chrétiens aux premiers siècles de l'église," *Esprit et vie* 83 (1973) 87-91.

15. Meyendorff, *Marriage* 10.

16. Henri de Lubac, *Corpus Mysticum* (Paris: Aubier, 1944) 255-284; Marie-Dominique Chenu, *La Théologie au douzième siècle* (Paris: J. Vrin, 1957) 159-209.

17. Thomas Aquinas, *Summa Theologiae*, III, Suppl., q. 65, 1. Michael G. Lawler challenges this particular Thomistic point in *Secular Marriage, Christian Sacrament* (Mystic, CT: Twenty-Third Publications, 1985) 68-77. Aquinas understood marriage in the "genus of sign," sign of grace, and one of the seven sacraments, against the objection of some contemporary theologians: "Matrimony, since it has pleasure annexed to it, does not conform man to Christ's passion, which was painful and therefore it is not a sacrament" (Suppl., q. 42, a.1, Praet. 3).

18. Bernard J. Cooke, *Sacraments and Sacramentality* (Mystic, CT: Twenty-Third Publications, 1983) 20.

19. In his mystical theology Hugh of St. Victor speaks of the bond of love and the communion of hearts as the essence of marriage; see Joseph Fuchs, "Marital Love, Christian Pluralism in the 12th Century," *Theology Digest* 33 (1986) 313-318.

20. See Andrés Manrique, "El Matrimonio, praxis del cristianismo primitivo," *Biblia y Fe* 12 (1986) 325-340.

21. *Lumen Gentium* 11.

22. Denis O'Callaghan, "Marriage as Sacrament," *Concilium* 55 (1970) 107.

23. See note 14 above.

24. G. Martinez, "Marriage as Worship: A Theological Analogy," *Worship* 62 (1988) 352-353 (reprinted as chapter 1 of this volume).

25. Giuseppe Baldanza, "Il matrimonio come sacramento perma-

nente," In *Realtà e valori del sacramento del matrimonio: Convegno di aggiornamento, Roma [...], 1-4 novembre 1975*, ed. Achille M. Triacca and Giovanni Pianazzi (Rome: Libreria Ateneo Salesiano, 1976) 102.

26. *Gaudium et Spes* 48.

27. See in this regard Kenneth Stevenson, *To Join Together: The Rite of Marriage* (New York: Pueblo, 1987) 3-24; Chauvet, "Le Mariage" 99-105.

28. O'Callaghan, "Marriage as Sacrament" 104.

29. David M. Thomas, *Christian Marriage: A Journey Together* (Wilmington: M. Glazier, 1983) 203.

30. Kasper, *Theology of Christian Marriage* 27.

31. Augustine, *De Bono Coniugali* 7.7; *De Nuptiis et Concupiscentia* I, ch. 17, no. 19.

32. Karl Rahner, "Marriage as a Sacrament," *Theology Digest* 17 (1969) 7.

33. As the International Theological Commission states: "The strength and greatness of the grace of Christ are extended to all people . . . This legitimate marriage has its authentic goodness and values . . . [which] come from God the creator and make them share—in an inchoate way—in the marital love which unites Christ with his Church" (Prop, 3.4 in Malone and Connery, eds., *Contemporary Perspectives* 22).

34. *Gaudium et Spes* 11.

35. Karl Lehmann, "Christian Marriage as Sacrament," *Communio* 6 (1979) 14-21.

36. A valid marriage contract between baptized persons is always a sacrament, according to Canon 1055. This principle, if applied in a generalized way, seems rather simplistic, because "the absence of personal faith compromises the validity of the sacrament" (International Theological Commission, prop. 2.3).

37. Louis Villette applies to marriage what Thomas Aquinas states in regard to faith and penance: "faith makes the penitential acts of the person the valid matter of the sacrament" (*Foi et sacrement*, vol. 2, *De saint Thomas à Karl Barth* [Paris: Bloud et Gay, 1964] 55-56).

38. *Gaudium et Spes* 48.

39. Matthias Joseph Scheeben, *The Mysteries of Christianity* (St. Louis: B. Herder, 1946) 601, n. 13. The work of this nineteenth-century German theologian still remains profound and modern.

40. Speaking from the consideration of this baptismal character, Wood rightly points out in regard to a non-sacramental marriage of a Christian that "to choose not to participate in God's grace in a sacramental marriage is not a choice in freedom but symptomatic of the distance from true freedom" ("The Marriage of Baptized Unbelievers" 291).

# THE CELEBRATION

# 5

## Marriage as Initiatory Sacrament: The Making of a Vocation

THE FORMING OF AN INTIMATE PARTNERSHIP AND FAMILY IS INCONceivable without a dynamic process in which man and woman separate from their original families, build a shared world, and commit to one another for life. In practice this process entails a transitional period of two different stages: the engagement and the wedding. The first stage, in which ideally male and female experience physical attraction, become intimate friends, and see a future of bonding and growth together, is normally formalized with the engagement. Despite the fact that this period of engagement (if there is one nowadays) has always been culturally conditioned and has undergone radical changes in our time, it remains an important stage of the preparation process to marriage.

From the religious perspective, these initiatory aspects are the first and basic phase of the pastoral dimension of marriage. Unfortunately, the traditionally longer process of family, social, and religious preparations for marriage has been reduced to a bare minimum. Thus the church should respond to the spiritual needs (the connection between faith and sacrament) as well as the human maturity (relational skills and conjugal qualities) with a support system for the passage from single into married life. This initiatory process is the entrance into a lifelong journey of both a human experience and a religious reality, and does not end with the wedding liturgy, and consequently is an integral part of the sacramentality of marriage.

This new understanding of the proximate preparation for the vocation of conjugal life makes marriage an initiatory sacrament in its own right. As in the case of all sacraments, marriage has to be rooted in baptismal and paschal foundations. Sacramental initiation is the process of symbolic actions by which faith empowers us and leads us into the mystery. It is a process of conversion and formation which, in the case of marriage, responds to the many-sided aspects of the vital bond that cements the interpersonal communion and the parental and public vocation of the future family. The profound changes of the social patterns of today's marriage in our post-Christian world are asking, in fact, for a radical—hopefully also realistic—new approach to the pastoral care of marriage celebration. Consequently, the solemnization of the wedding in church (stage of incorporation) is not enough, because it is only part of that longer process of the making of the marital vocation.

Within the current crisis in the stability of marriage and the need for a new integration of its reality and values into a contemporary Christian synthesis, it is important to understand the dynamics of the religious initiatory process of the specific vocation of marriage. Grace cannot operate apart from the reality and dynamics of our actual existence. Ideally, this process effects the transition through the liminal stage and the final testing period of engagement into a developing and healthy relationship.

What follows will focus on ritual and culture and will consider marriage from this perspective of sacramental initiation, retracing the constants of the Christian tradition, and inquiring the cultural patterns and social forces which today condition the prospect and actual realization of the marital vocation. Consequently, this chapter will be a study of the scope and practice of ritualizing the stages of marriage celebration; the historical traditions of ritual initiation; and the problems of the relationship of modern culture vis à vis the rituals of marriage initiation.

## RITES OF PASSAGE TODAY

A true ritualization embracing the whole reality of Christian partnership should have a real impact on the configuration and outcome of the life of the couple. Experience shows that for the majority of young people of this generation, the sacramental celebration of marriage remains a marginal religious experience. It does not significantly influence the personal attitudes and social character of the shared values and identity of the Christian couple. After the church wedding, life goes on as before, because there is no concrete realization of the sacramentality of marriage and, consequently, no concrete living out of its conjugal spirituality. The rite is there: what is missing is the spirit. There is no spirit because there is no preparation that is integral to the sacramental process. In fact, in the case of marriage the process of ritual passage and faith preparation for adulthood have been lost.

Only recently has the church acknowledged the need for the pastoral and the spiritual development of the family during the life cycle.[1] In the past, marriage preparation was based on remedial and preventive concepts consisting of a pre-nuptial investigation, determination of the readiness for marriage and an interview. The new approach toward marriage preparation is based on a personal encounter with other couples and story-telling about one's own family and faith experiences. But for the most part, and despite the existence of multi-disciplinary programs and the excellent work of different marriage movements (like Marriage Encounter), there are no comprehensive initiation processes into the meaning and values of forming another conjugal community and family, and a follow-up pastoral support system for the younger families.[2]

An initiation process is needed, not only because the relationship cycle of engagement towards marriage is a significant transitional stage of life, but mainly because the old cultural supports and social customs of the past generation (the art of courtship, traditional value-complexes, and family involvement) to a great extent have been lost. This is an opportunity for the church to create an effective process of marriage preparation which should provide for a true conjugal community of life and faith. Since this process involves a human stage of development that goes beyond ecclesiastical competencies, marriage preparation should include important insights from the perspective of the human sciences.

### Insights of Human Sciences

Erik Erikson's theory of psycho-social development is helpful in understanding the stage of the young adulthood crisis of "intimacy versus isolation." He stresses the importance of keeping healthy tensions, tensions needed for developing a mature capacity for love shared in intimate relationships and lifetime commitments. "The lack of proper resolution of this conflict," John Elias comments, "leads to an isolated existence wherein persons are unable to make needed intimate contacts or close friends."[3] Erikson's theoretical understanding of human development include his insights concerning the reaffirmation (against Freud) of ritual behavior for healthy human growth. Genuine psycho-social maturity, self-identity, and a communal shared vision hinge on a healthy ritualization of human experience.[4]

Cultural anthropology is another important avenue of the understanding the function of human ritualization. The seminal work of Arnold van Gennep, Les Rites de Passage, became a landmark which guided other research in the understanding of the traditional life cycle rituals of birth, puberty, marriage, and death.[5] He provided a model of the rites of initiation into a community and its cultural values consisting in a triple pattern of Rites of Separation, Rites of Liminality, and Rites of Incorporation. Their function is to provide meaning, to integrate into a community, to realize the transformation, and to symbolize the originality of the new life.

The application of Van Gennep's insights to marriage, which were subsequently developed by Victor Turner,[6] is obvious. They can be applied not only to the key sacramental moments of life, but also to the critical area of marriage and family life celebrations. The loss of the awareness and the dynamics of these profound structures of the human growth and interaction leads to the crisis of the sacramental symbolism which responds to these profound structures.

*Deep Structures of Marriage*

Marriage is a rite of initiation in its own right. Its relational nature, complex meanings, and challenging realities span from the first moment of the increasing intimate relationship of two people to the different stages of the marriage journey. The Anglican scholar Kenneth Stevenson is right in insisting that those three stages are the "deep structures" of marriage.[7] Marriage involves the different stages of preparation for the celebration of the wedding and growth of the formed partnership, especially in the early years, and it needs to be looked at from the perspective of van Gennep's typology of rites.[8]

Although they are not always equally developed, this process of a triple pattern is a constant in primitive societies and in the formal marriage customs of primitive Judaism. In the tradition of ancient Christianity, van Gennep's ritual stages are more explicitly evident in the eastern and in the Hispanic rites of Medieval Spain. The rites of separation are the *betrothal*, which involves a provisional commitment to a future marriage. The rites of *liminality* correspond to the engagement period, of preparation which climaxes in the rite of *incorporation* of the wedding celebration.

These stages of the relational cycle have always been part of the preparation for marriage, albeit, as stated above, in a complex variety of personal, social, and religious styles. They correspond to the basic patterns of the "larger secular rituals" of marriage celebration in all societies. On the contrary, in contemporary western cultures, interpersonal relationships tend to become a private affair experienced in isolation by the couple. The split and fragmentation between the human and religious, the public and private spheres cannot nurture a commitment to communal symbols and shared values.[9]

Despite this cultural atmosphere of distrust and ambivalence toward the institutional and communal dimension of any interpersonal relationship, the need for healthy ritualization and religious support will always be required by the natural ambiguity of an in-between stage of engagement toward a conjugal community which is necessarily public. In fact, engaged couples wrestle with the ambiguities and tensions of blurring and shifting traditional male and female roles. They go through a period of testing areas of compatibility and adjustment, and of an increasingly intimate relationship for a lifetime commitment. In this liminal state, ritualizing can be seen from the perspective of two important functions of rituals: "a mechanism of continuity, a way of countering change" and also, "affording change via adaptation or integration."[10]

## A Phased Initiation

The church can provide the appropriate environment of a welcoming and supporting community of discernment and counseling, faith development and initiation into a conjugal spirituality. However, this goal requires a shift of mentality and style from the old model of a remedial and doctrinal program into the new one of a living experience in a phased initiation, beginning with engagement and continuing through the first years of marriage. Kenneth Stevenson supports "a three-stage marriage liturgy to be inaugurated, not as an optional extra, but *as the norm* from which shorter versions of the scheme could derive their existence."[11] The purpose is not to resurrect anachronistic customs, but to regain the spiritual roots of the biblical and Christian tradition of a "marriage in the Lord" in a post-Christian-society. This return to the sources is certainly needed despite the fact that in the ancient tradition it was not the official church, but the family which celebrated those marriage rituals. The church, in fact, already provided its rites of Christian initiation, the foundational sacramentality and spirituality of a Christian marriage, which we are beginning to rediscover today.

The recently restored Rite of Christian Initiation of Adults (RCIA) is therefore the theological model and the ritual framework of a three-stage preparation and celebration of marriage. Pope John Paul II echoed this new departure in the dynamic understanding of marriage when he envisioned its preparation as a "journey of faith, which is similar to the catechumenate,"[12] and the pastoral care of the family as a progressive action "step by step in the different stages of its formation and development."[13] This new framework became apparent after the council envisioned the new rite of initiation (RCIA) which is the best fruit of the liturgical reform.

Various national conferences of bishops, like the American bishops, recommended that the implementation of a similar journey of faith and conversion be applied to the marriage preparation process.[14] This journey has the following rationale and components: (1) it is a *gradual process* marked in ritual stages of a journey of conversion to Christ in living a relationship—flexibility and adaptation in its implementation are important; (2) it presupposes *communitarian participation*, especially through the support of the inspirational models of a sponsor couple—in a new understanding of the parish as a ministerial community, lay men and women have crucial roles to play; (3) it is *scripturally and liturgically centered*, and includes the human values of marriage.

Both aspects, the formative and the catechetical, are stressed by the revised rite of marriage issued in 1990. In fact, the biblico-liturgical contents provide a "catechesis dynamically oriented to the celebration, constantly enriched with liturgical contents, fundamentally and primarily structured on liturgical rites, and effectively leading to a Christian conjugal life."[15] The content of this integrated experience of marriage initiation responds to the uniqueness of each engaged couple, values human experience, and provides a critical view of current social reality from the spirit of the Gospels.

Such a process, as an integrated unity which attempts a serious initiation into the complex realities of marriage and personal faith conversion, should provide the sacramental support needed for married life.

Despite the enormous progress made from the doctrinal and canonical points of view, and the success of the two new Roman rites of marriage (issued in 1969 and 1990), the church experiences difficulty in making this renewal appreciated, and in confronting the current crisis of marriage. Therefore, today's new integration of human and Christian values cannot happen without a truthful ritual process of marriage preparation and support. This initiation process is, in fact, integral not only to the anthropological complexities of marriage, but also to its sacramental nature.

## TRADITIONS OF RITUAL INITIATION

In approaching critically the historical traditions, we can draw on the lessons of history and determine future directions, especially in regard to the initiation process and ritual expressions of marriage. This goal is needed in order to respond to one of the main goals of Vatican II's Constitution on the Sacred Liturgy in regard to invigorating a Christian ritual which meets the needs of modern times.[16]

Actually, this consciousness of the importance of the ritual framework for human and faith growth is even stronger today. The following quotation sums up this importance in the case of the family rites of passage:

> At the heart of faith formation is participation in the Church's rites and sacramental life. John Westerhoff has written, "When we ask, what is most significant in the shaping of *faith . . . character* (a people's sense of identity and their disposition to behave in particular ways), and *consciousness* (a people's attitudes and awareness), the answer is the rituals and ceremonials of a people's primary community. These symbolic actions, words, and behaviors, which express and manifest the community's sacred narrative, significantly influence a people's faith and life. There is tremendous formative influence inherent in ritual ceremonial practices and experiences."[17]

The ritualization of marriage as a rite of passage, which is an integral part of both the transition to a new stage of life and the sacramental process, has the potential for shaping the faith of the couple and revitalizing enduring values.

The celebration of the process of marrying, throughout history and in all civilizations, offers us the clearest argument regarding the intrinsic link between culture and ritual. Since the rites of marriage have—to a great extent—been fragmented or lost in modern culture, there is much we can learn from an understanding of the basic anthropological connection between the "cult" and culture of marriage. From the beginning, Christianity was open to whatever ceremonies and festivities surrounding the joining of the two parties and the two families were expressed in the local social practices of the ritual passage of marriage; but it always tried to preserve the biblical ideals and respond to the pastoral needs of the day, because a

Christian marriage had to be a marriage "in the Lord" (1 Cor 7:39). On this we will expand next, highlighting the main features of the Christian tradition already studied in the chapter on "History and Its Lessons."

### Historical Traditions

From the historical perspective of Christian liturgy, we can draw three principles from an *a posteriori* reflection on the intense period of religious-cultural interaction and inculturation extending mostly from the third- to sixth-century Christianity. These are elimination, assimilation, and reinterpretation, and apply to the interaction between Christianity and the existing rituals of the Greco-Roman marriage.

The celebration of marriage in the Greco-Roman culture consisted of two major parts: the engagement before marriage and the rites of marriage itself. The engagement before marriage appears in the third century clearly distinct from marriage, but important from a social and juridical point of view.[18] It took place in the context of a meal. There was a formal promise of the husband to receive the girl into his house; reading of the pacts of the dowry with reciprocal exchange of gifts; the presentation of the nuptial ring by the groom to the bride, and sometimes the presentation of the dowry, as well as the mutual kiss (a custom introduced in a later period to ratify the nuptial promise and which had a juridical weight).

The nuptial ceremony, which lasted more than one day, was a sacred and family rite, consisting essentially of three stages: the presentation of the girl, the procession to the household, and the rite in the house of the husband. The ceremony was eminently religious and revolved around the divinities of the household.

It is important to observe that the celebration of marriage was a process in stages which included the separate rites of betrothal or engagement. This celebration had a prominently sacred character, though the legal procedure based on the reciprocal consent of the pair was essential.[19] It presented a balance of human and symbolic gestures from which the rite of Christian marriage derived, to a great extent, as far as the basic symbolism is concerned. The advent of Christianity coin-

cided with a period of secularization of the matrimonial ceremonies. Christianity completed this process of desacralization
of the rite, as far as the Gentile household rites was concerned,
and also regarding the temple of the divinities.

There is no trace of a Christian ritual ceremony or ecclesiastical intervention in the early church. But the Christian spirit
refused to accept certain elements of specific pagan religions
(for instance, idolatrous sacrifice) or practices that were considered licentious. Tertullian in the third century opposed the
common use of the crown of flowers for Christian women.[20]
To marry a pagan meant to be crowned idolatrously with him,
and therefore, to fall into idolatry.

This brief historical survey shows that the household ritual
of the Greco-Roman marriage in early Christian centuries,
phased, deeply religious and symbolic, depended entirely on
their folk tradition and beliefs. The early Christian approach
did not try to sacralize existing cultural forms, but respected
the family process of the marriage passage within the framework of Christian inculturation: the incarnation or assimilation of cultural and social elements, and the elimination of
specific cultic elements which were in blatant contrast with the
fundamentally covenantal Judeo-Christian concept.[21]

This Christian inculturation of different symbolic acts of the
pre-Christian marriage ritual is a fact beginning at the end of
the third century.[22] The formalization of engagement (betrothal) in Rome remains essential, but limited to the domestic
and social context. From the beginning, though, Christians certainly informally ritualized the different stages towards the
formation of a new hearth, and did so with a Christian spirit
and prayer. A liturgy of marriage began to develop after the
fourth century in Rome. This type of sacramental blessing (not
solemnization) of the bridal pair, attested in the Verona, Gelasian and Gregorian sacramentaries (fifth to seventh centuries)
was only an expression of the church's pastoral care, not juridical appropriation.

Fully respectful of the structure of marriage as family affair
and integrated in the process of the local folk traditions, the
church limited its intervention for the first millennium to the
liturgical blessing. However, the west never developed a rich
theology of marriage, as was true for the Orthodox Churches

of the east. Moreover, some of these Churches always had a separate liturgical rite of betrothal. Their ancient tradition provides an eloquent example of rich symbolism and doctrinally profound formulas of prayer that we could well emulate. In both east and west, Christians always respected the paternal authority regarding marriage and the familial and secular frame of the entire celebration of the wedding until its transfer to the church building. This transfer was initiated in Northern France during the eleventh century.

Throughout the Middle Ages the new ecclesiastical ceremonies subsumed and reduced the separate formal customs of the marriage stages (engagement and wedding) which in the past had taken place in the house of the bride. The result was a gradual breakdown of the process of ritualizing marriage, consummated in the Roman Ritual (published in 1614) of the legalistic Tridentine reform, and a future cleavage between secular and ecclesiastical celebrations. Within the patriarchal household, Christian marriage had always expressed itself in a great variety of models of behavior, understanding of personal roles, and views of sexual relationships within the local cultures—Roman, Celtic, Hispanic, Germanic. Likewise, their liturgical rituals of celebration always resisted the process of Roman unification. In fact, some local rituals (as in France and Spain) continued the betrothal blessing in the post-Tridentine period.

The Protestant Reformation emphasized the holiness of marriage and family, albeit not from the sacramental perspective, which was denied, but from a renewed theology of the Christian vocation and the covenantal nature of God's plan for the couple. Protestant rituals continued the Middle Ages traditions and remained important religious celebrations.[23]

In the sixteenth century the Council of Trent recognized the validity and importance of particular rituals, as did the liturgical reform of Vatican II in our century. Not only local customs and ceremonies should be retained, but even more, each national church could "draw up its own rite suited to the usages of place and people." Again, Vatican II gives us a clue in a general principle of adaptation: "From the customs and traditions of their people, from their arts and science, Christian life can be accommodated to the genius and the dispositions of each culture."[24] As for the rite of betrothal, the *Book of Blessings* of 1984 contains an "Order for the Blessing of an Engaged Couple."

### Ritual Initiation

From the historical traditions we can learn a constant within the long evolution of the changing historical patterns of marriage: the symbolic celebration of its entire passage from the moment of engagement to the moment of incorporation into a new family. Usually the family has been the primary provider of a support system, punctuated formally or informally by rituals. This historical constant demonstrates that the ritualization of this most important stage of the life cycle is primarily an anthropological reality having the potential to nurture the human maturity needed for a stable conjugal partnership. In seeking a new integration of faith values in each historical period, Christians adopted the current social customs supporting the couple in the years-long transition to a stable family.

This support system of family rituals and customs from courtship into marriage were evidently initiatory. Marriage itself was a holy state to the people of a baptismal experience of God, and thus considered sacramental, albeit not in the technical and restricted sense of the ecclesiastical wedding ceremony established after the twelfth century. Referring to this later development of the sacramental status and initiatory nature of the marriage rite, J. Martos states:

> Wedding ceremonies are always sacramental, at least in the broad sense of being celebrations of the sacred value of marriage, whatever it may be in a given culture, as well as in the sense of being rituals of initiation to a new style of life which is honored and meaningful, supported by social custom and religious tradition. In these same ways Christian wedding ceremonies have always been sacramental, for they have celebrated the sacred value of marriage in a Christian culture, and they have initiated men and women into a style of life that was to be modeled on the relationship between Christ and the church.[25]

Any approach to the problem of marriage today must take into account its complex reality, which comprises interpersonal and social, familial and ecclesial relationships. Marriage is a human and social event of a lifelong journey. We cannot reduce its complex reality to a strict matter of ritual, or even to the planning period of the wedding; nor can we limit it to the specifically spiritual or moral considerations. This complex reality is asking for a process oriented support system capable of molding Christian patterns of social life.

In past generations marriage and family life were supported by the social structures of the community itself, but today a gap exists between Christian values and cultural patterns. The success of the ritual celebration of Christian marriage depends on the larger context of pastoral care that starts with the process of Christian initiation (baptism-confirmation-eucharist) and continues with an adequate process of marriage formation. Historians of liturgy stress the importance of this overall picture of the order of worship as the real matrix of personal conversion and social transformation. The following statement of Josef Jungmann in reference to the sacramental life of ancient Christianity applies to a great extent to our contemporary situation: "Society, political life, the life of the people, family life, the position of the woman, the respect of human dignity—be it slave, child or even the unborn—all this was transformed by a slow but sure process of fermentation: from a pagan society a Christian society was born."[26]

In today's foundering secular culture, sacramentality understood in a broader way will play the decisive role in this renewal of the complex reality of marriage. The imaginative renewal of the sacramental catechesis and faith formation, ritual symbolism and scriptural basis of marriage should explore and celebrate the lay and family vocation today with all its complex dimensions. This imaginative renewal should express the full dimensions of a fleshly love and great sacrament. As J.D. Crichton says:

> Marriage may be regarded as the archetypal case of the coinherence of the divine and the human. Here is human love, earthly, warm, and rich with every kind of fleshly association which yet reaches beyond itself to a total self-giving. It is this love that two people bring to God, and in the encounter that ensues God's love meets and transfuses them so that, henceforth, they are able to love each other with a love in which God is creatively present. Nonetheless, their love remains fully hu-

man and yet at the same time is the sacrament-sign of their covenanted love as it is also the means by which they and their love are sanctified."[27]

While the sacramentally celebrated human and divine realities of love and fidelity are universal, the symbolic models (like vocation, or communion) that support and reflect them are not. The sensibility and creativity regarding language and symbolic models and their social perception vary according to epoch and culture. What unifies the local varieties of historical and present rituals is the ecclesial expression of the same Christocentric faith, as Kenneth Stevenson beautifully puts it:

> Marriage rites in Christianity are a rich tapestry, woven with care and love and creativity. They speak of the things of the kingdom of God in the differing ways in which the central relationship of humanity has been, is and will continue to be experienced within the Body of Christ. It is a story of humankind restored and forgiven, lost and loved, resolute to undertake a commitment to live together, "in sickness and in health," as prophetic sign of the new creation which Christ "adorned and beautified" at Cana.[28]

In conclusion, Christian tradition teaches us two important lessons: first, the initiatory nature of the entire marriage passage (anthropological reality); secondly, the sacramental nature of the marital union and life as a whole (theological reality), originating not from the wedding rite itself, but from the baptismal consecration of the bridal pair. The gradual divorce between marriage family rituals and the church wedding of the last centuries "led to a secularization of the domestic and its alienation from the realm of the sacred, now identified with the church," state two experts of the historical marriage rites. They rightly affirm that "the renewal of Christian marriage, then, would seem to be inseparable, finally, from the renewal of baptismal consciousness and from the profound consequences that will flow therefrom not only for the life of the family, but for the structures of the Church itself. Thus we shall have come full circle, back to the baptismal foundations of 'marriage in Christ' with which the Church's theology of marriage began."[29]

The pastoral wisdom of the church, the key to every historical renewal and its ritual expression for twenty centuries, and
the varied symbolic models of the Christian traditions provide
the necessary experience to revive the initiatory process of
marriage vocation beyond the formalism and reductionism of
the legalistic approach of the last centuries. This varied heri-
tage of historical traditions was enriched a hundredfold by the
complementary models that emerged from Vatican II, namely,
covenant, communion, and vocation. The new national rituals
that will follow the second typical edition of the Roman rite of
1990 are the best hope of a truly spiritual and festive, ecclesial
and social marriage ministry and celebration in critical interaction with modern cultures.

## RITUAL INCULTURATION AND MODERN CULTURE

The relevance of a ritual is necessarily tied to the real-life
experience of the people. Thus the process of marrying is tied
to the personal and social factors that shape the contemporary
understanding of marriage. Every person and every couple
have their own particular background (personal, life-realities
and relationships) within the family, and a great variety of cultural influences. Marriage is, in fact, a historical and dynamic
reality that cannot happen apart from the concrete personal
and social experience of two people. Consequently, the social
and religious reality of marriage is always new, as is the personal reality of the shared love and commitment celebrated in
the sacrament of marriage. As Gerard Fourez says, "the reality
of the sacrament is the real-life family experience itself, which
is looked at as the sign of God's alliance with the people and
of the fidelity of Christ and the Church."[30]
The relationship between ritual and life appears even
stronger when we look at the broader context of the human
meaning and components of a couple's relationship and the
celebration of their partnership. Before being a religious phenomenon, marriage is essentially a human mystery, like the
many-faceted realities of love. In its profound values (intimate
loving and procreativity, serving each other, tenderness and
mutual respect), it is already in itself a saving reality embodied in the human mystery of an intimate partnership.

*Religious Ritual and Social Reality*

The religious solemnization is only part of the traditional "rituals" that initiate two people into a committed partnership. While celebrating the human experience of love and the Christian ideals of a relationship grounded in the liberating love of Christ, the sacramental process cannot be seen as unrelated to the customary and informal rites of passage. A broader consideration of the many-sided reality of marriage (psychological and social, cultural and familiar, spiritual and ecclesial) is important in approaching the relevance of the celebration of the sacrament. There is, too often, a cleavage between the real life and faith experience of people and the high standards of religious content of sacramental marriage.

The human experience of reality is mediated by culture, and in the case of marriage, sociobehavioral facts condition its human potential.[31] Thus, today it has become a truism to say that the crisis of marriage is primarily cultural. It is cultural in nature because, to a great extent, our secular and individualistic culture provides the value systems in which a couple lives out human expectations and religious commitments. Their relationship and family life is configured and conditioned socially, financially, and culturally.

The complexity of ideas, values, beliefs, and capabilities which determine our way of being and living constitute our common culture. As Vatican II states, "the human person can achieve full humanity only by means of culture."[32] The council's understanding of the rightful autonomy of modern culture and its secular order is positive and critical and it is aware that profound changes brought about "a new age of human history."[33] This new age and culture struck the old foundations of family structure, its economic conditions and moral values as an earthquake strikes an old village. From the floundering of the old marriage institution arose a new cultural consciousness in our modern society.

The consequences of this new situation of marriage are a new *kairos*, or time of grace, for the church. Its role of evangelization and sacramental celebration is not to salvage the anachronistic patterns of marriage, which are not linked to faith, but to critically transform the new cultural mediation. Since the cultural supports of the old patterns of a religious marriage protected by the church have changed, a new dialogue and symbiosis is needed between faith and culture, specifically between the Christian meaning of marriage and the secular wisdom of married people.[34]

A modern Christian vision is needed in order to let marriage be a credible institution of personal and social fulfillment, and also an actual saving reality in the midst of today's secular life. In a secular society the evangelization of new models of marriage will require a long process of inculturation of Christian values, and although this process of critical interaction with culture cannot be reduced to the ritual of marriage, ritual understood in a broader way is an integral part of this process.

This process should begin with a new awareness of the shifting social reality of the contemporary family, which in the words of Pope John Paul II, "has been beset by the many profound and rapid changes that have affected society and culture."[35] In western culture, these fundamental changes developed in the early 1960s, reached a peak in the 1970s, and stabilized in the 1980s. The family picture will never be the same again.[36]

It is easier to summarize the confirmed patterns provided by current sociological research than to understand the complex dynamics operative in the relationship between contemporary secular culture and marriage. There is no simple explanation for the profound crisis of family identity within contemporary culture.

The functions of the family have been changed by the shifting structures of society itself. The family is subject to the enormous mobility and plurality of life-styles which characterize modern society. A predominantly industrial and urban society has resulted in the loss of the social and productive functions of the extended family of the past. In sociological terms, the family was de-institutionalized, which brought about lesser credibility for the marital institution and a lack of social support. The family has become an almost exclusively economic entity whose function is to be a consumer of goods.

On the positive side, there has been more emphasis on the priority given to the personal values of mutual caring and trust, communication and sharing within a relation based on intimate companionship and love. For some, a shift of roles took place from a perceived functional and instrumental subordination within the old family system into a personalist and interdependent relationship of the modern nuclear family. Hence the new roles of mutuality and equality that characterize relationships in the life style of some modern couples.

On the negative side, this primacy of personalism has created a pervasive individualism and privatism that reduces the person to a *homo consumens*. The family suffers the consequence of this exaggerated individualism and fragmentation.

Without pretending to give a comprehensive view of current issues and complexities, the following outline summarizes the crucial factors shaping modern families. Personalization established a new conjugal relationship, especially in the role of equality of the woman in all dimensions. This personalization demands more open and spontaneous relations and commitment to mutual growth through communication and intimacy. The biological control of procreation drastically changed the view of sexuality and broadened the concept of generativity. The relational dimensions of sexual intercourse consequently resulted in smaller family units. Longevity, mobility, and expectations of the spouses made marriage an unpredictable life journey of reoccurring adjustments.

All these related factors brought about new possibilities for human fulfillment, but also greater moral challenges. Statistics on divorce, unmarried cohabitation, abortion, and so on, are signs of a "disturbing degradation of some fundamental values."[37]

Following the analysis of social critics like Gibson Winter, and Robert Bellah[38] there seems to be a consensus among many authors concerning the fact that "individualism, it appears, is at the very core of the American soul"[39] and that "our world view and ethos now reflect a kind of 'ontological individualism' in which the individual has a kind of primary reality.[40] Sociologist John Naisbitt noted in the 1980s that "the basic building block of society is shifting from the family to the individual."[41] Without a balanced conception and an actual experience of the social and communal dimensions of the person, these individualistic trends will neither cement life-styles of stability and solidarity in marriage, nor can they provide the meaning of a communal sacramental experience.

## A Christian Response

In our rapidly changing society, the conjugal community, and in a broader sense, the family, are still in search of an identity. Since Christianity is transcultural and marriage is historical, there is not one model, but many models of Christian families. This is especially true in the United States with its multicultural and pluralistic society.

The bishops of the United States responded to these challenges with three fundamental principles basic to a balanced conception of the family: (1) the primary community of family is essential for the maturity of the individual; (2) there needs to be an intrinsic connection between families and society for a sense of social solidarity; (3) the church needs the family, in which intimacy, interdependence, and religious socialization develop.[42]

It is obvious that there is a need to create new models of Christian identity, new domestic churches characterized by openness to the permanent values of modernity consistent with the Christian faith; equality without the loss of individuality; personalization based on the principle of love of community as well as a person; a critical attitude toward our consumer and hedonistic society characterized by a life style of simplicity and human dignity; and the value of sexuality as endowed with creative and unitive dimensions. The papal document on the family emphasizes four general tasks for the family: (1) to form a community of persons; (2) to serve life; (3) to participate in society's development; (4) and to share in the life and mission of the church.[43]

* * * * * * * * * *

Personal and social transformation can only happen through a process of conversion and rebirth. By means of word and symbol, sacramental spirituality provides the radical death and resurrection pattern and the Christian dynamism needed for the transformation of our impoverished secularized modern culture. Marriage passage with all its stages is an essential time for the experience of that sacramental spirituality which asks for ritualization "in spirit and in truth."

*Notes*

1. *Familiaris Consortio* 65.

2. Document issued by the Bishop's Committee for Pastoral Research and Practices, National Council of Catholic Bishops, *Faithful To Each Other Forever: A Catholic Handbook of Pastoral Help for Marriage Preparation* (Washington, D.C.: United States Catholic Conference, 1989).

3. Scholarly work by John L. Elias, *Moral Education: Secular and Religious* (Malabar, FL: Krieger Publishing Co., 1989) 74.

4. Erik Erikson, *Toys and Reasons: Stages in the Ritualization of Experience* (New York: W.W. Norton and Co., 1977). A synthesis of important psychological and religious insights based on the theories of Piaget, Kohlberg, and others is presented in Robert Kegan's essay, "There the Dance Is; Religious Dimensions of a Developmental Framework," in Christiane Brusselmans, ed., *Toward Moral and Religious Maturity* (Morristown, NJ: Silver Burdett and Co., 1980) 403-440.

5. Originally published in 1909, Arnold van Gennep, *Rites of Passage* (Reissued by University of Chicago Press, 1981) 10-11.

6. Victor Turner, *The Ritual Process* (London: Routledge and Kegan Paul, 1969) 94-165. For a contemporary appreciation of Turner's theories of ritual study, see Mary Collins, *Worship: Renewal To Practice* (Washington, D.C.: The Pastoral Press, 1987) 59-71.

7. Turner, *The Ritual Process* 7-10.

8. For a contemporary understanding of the rites of passage, see Arnold Niederer, "Eléments de ritualité dans la vie," in Pierre Centlivres et Jacques Hainard, *Le Rites de passage aujourd'hui* (Lausanne: Editions L'Age d'Homme, 1986) 172.

9. See William R. Crockett, "Le Christianisme et la culture dans la société moderne sécularisée," *La Maison-Dieu* 179 (1989) 45-56.

10. Catherine Bell, "Ritual, Change, and Changing Rituals," *Worship* 63 (1989) 33.

11. Kenneth Stevenson, *To Join Together: The Rite of Marriage* (New York: Pueblo Press, 1987) 192.

12. *Familiaris Consortio*, p. 66. There is a trend in the Eastern Churches toward restoration of ritualization of betrothal at the time of engagement; for example, Diocese of St. Maron, U.S.A., Office of Liturgy, *The Mystery of Crowning* (Washington, D.C., 1985) 3-9.

13. *Familiaris Consortio* 65.

14. The first documented mention of the application of RCIA (Rite of Christian Initiation of Adults) to marriage preparation is in the pastoral of the Italian bishops on "Marriage and Family Today in Italy," (11-15-1969); see Luca Brandolini, "Catechesi matrimoniale rinnovata: catecumenato al Sacramento del Matrimonio," in A.M. Triacca and G. Pianazzi, *Realtà e valori del sacramento del matrimonio* (Rome, LAS, 1976) 431-445. The U.S. Bishop's Committee on Pastoral Research and Practices provides guidelines for development and the ingredients of the RCIA for an integrated process of marriage preparation, *Faithful to Each Other Forever*, pp. 65-66. This idea was considered by other Catholic Conferences; see Christopher J. Walsh and G. Steel, "La Revision du rite catholique de marriage pour L'Angleterre et le Pays de Galles," *La Maison-Dieu* 179 (1989) 99-110.

15. Archille M. Triacca, "Spiritus Sancti Virtutis Infusio: A proposito di alcune tematiche teologico liturgiche testimoniate nell' 'Editio Altera' dell' 'Ordo Celebrandi Matrimonium'," *Notitiae* 26 (1990) 386. Whether or not this new modern of marriage preparation and growth can be realistically implemented depends on many factors especially the parish ministers and the free cooperation of the couples. Practical suggestions of the preparation process through the ritualization of the three stages and symbolic liturgical enrichment are provided by Kenneth Stevenson, *To Join Together* 187-207. See also the excellent article of JoAnn Heaney-Hunter, "The RCIA: A Model for Marriage Preparation?" *Living Light* 27 (1991) 209-217.

I am indebted to Lawrence A. Hecker for letting me read his unpublished paper, "A Plan for a Marriage Preparation Process Based on The Rite of Christian Initiation of Adults," presented at the Graduate School of Religion and Religious Education, Fordham University, New York, 1989. He presents a theological-pastoral introduction and proposes a detailed plan which extends from the moment of pre-engagement till the first marriage anniversary.

16. Constitution on the Sacred Liturgy 4; see my article "Greco-Roman Cultural Symbols and Ritual Creativity Today: An Approach to Marriage," *Questions liturgiques* 65 (1984) 39-52.

17. John Roberto, "Foundational Principles for Faith Growth and Faith Sharing in Families," in John Roberto, ed., *Growing in Faith: A Catholic Family Sourcebook* (New Rochelle, NY: Don Bosco Multimedia, 1990).

18. From the verb "spondeo," "sponsalia," or the promise of marriage, with which the mutual consent was exchanged. This consent was almost equal juridically to a celebration of marriage.

19. Marriage could not be formalized by a sexual act but by a mutual consent; see Jean Evenou, "Marriage," in Aimé G. Martimort,

ed., *The Church at Prayer*, vol. 3, *The Sacraments* (Collegeville: The Liturgical Press, 1987) 185-207.

20. Tertullian, *De Corona*, 13, 4, and 14, 2 (CCL 1, 1061 and 1063).

21. Most researchers agree that there was no Christian liturgy for marriage at least before the fourth century. But Kenneth Stevenson thinks "that there was a marriage rite, that consisted of an adapted version of Jewish practice" (*To Join Together* 18).

22. Whereas Christians at first opposed the use of a garland, as we have seen in Tertullian, later on the Fathers of the Church will give to the same rite a Christian significance; for instance, John Chrysostom, Hom. 9 in 1 Tim. (PG 62:546); see Edward Schilliebeeckx, *Marriage, Human Reality, and Saving Mystery* (New York: Crossroad, 1986) 246-252.

23. See Thomas M. Martin, *The Challenge of Christian Marriage: Marriage in Scripture, History and Contemporary Life* (New York: Paulist Press, 1990) 92-101.

24. Decree on the Church's Missionary Activity 22 (Austin Flannery translation); see Constitution on the Sacred Liturgy 37. The inculturation of the marriage rite is a constant in the history of Christianity. There is quite an extensive bibliography on the contemporary problem of inculturation in many countries; see Anscar J. Chupungco, *Liturgies of the Future: The Process and Methods of Inculturation* (New York: Paulist Press, 1989) 101-149.

25. Joseph Martos, *Doors to the Sacred: A Historical Introduction to Sacraments in the Catholic Church* (Tarrytown, NY: Triumph Books, 1991) 386-387.

26. Josef A. Jungmann, *The Early Liturgy to the Time of Gregory the Great* (Notre Dame: University of Notre Dame Press, 1962) 165.

27. J.D. Crichton, "The Sacraments and Human Life," in *The Sacraments*, ed. M.J. Taylor (New York: Alba House, 1981) 34.

28. Kenneth W. Stevenson, *Nuptial Blessing: A Study of Christian Marriage Rites* (New York: Oxford University Press, 1983) 213.

29. Mark Searle and Kenneth W. Stevenson, *Documents of the Marriage Liturgy* (Collegeville: The Liturgical Press, 1992) 270-271.

30. Gerard Fourez, *Sacraments and Passages: Celebrating the Tensions of Modern Life* (Notre Dame: Ave Maria Press, 1981) 123. Another important insight of the sacramental reality of marriage is provided by James L. Empereur, who looks at it from the angle of liberation and justice, in J.L. Empereur and Christopher G. Kiesling, *The Liturgy That Does Justice* (Collegeville: The Liturgical Press, 1991) 179-201.

31. See Kathleen Fischer and Thomas Hart, "The Contemporary Setting For Marriage: Sociobehavioral Insights," in *Alternative Fu-*

*tures for Worship*, vol. 5, *Marriage* (Collegeville: The Liturgical Press, 1987) 15-32.

32. Pastoral Constitution on the Church in the Modern World 53 (Flannery 959).

33. Ibid. 54. The council document provides a definition of culture in *Gaudium and Spes* 53 and also a critique on the ambivalence of our modern culture, ibid. 5-9 (Flannery 906-909).

34. As Pope John Paul VI stated, "The split between the Gospel and culture is without a doubt the drama of our time" (*Evangelii Nuntiandi* 20).

35. *Familiaris Consortio* 1.

36. Many publications offer sociological data suggesting that there is a radical change in the marital and family structure in America. The United States has the highest rate of divorce in the western world, although the trend has stabilized since the 1980s. For a sociological analy*A Family Perspective in Church and Society: A Manual for All Pastoral Leaders* (Washington, D.C.: United States Catholic Conference, Office of Publishing and Promotion Services, 1988).

37. *Familiaris Consortio* 6.

38. Robert Bellah and others, *Habits of the Heart: Individualism and Commitment in American Life* (Berkley, CA: University of California Press, 1985); Gibson Winter, *Liberating Creation: Foundations of Religious Social Ethics* (New York: Crossroad, 1981); see also Christopher Lash, *The Culture of Narcissism: American Life in an Age of Diminishing Expectations* (New York: Warner Books, 1989). Similar cultural trends are felt in other industrial countries; see José M. Mardones, *Postmodernidad y cristianismo: El Desafío del fragmento* (Santander: Sal Terrae, 1988).

39. John Westerhoff, III, "Celebrating and Living the Eucharist: A Cultural Analysis," in Bernard J. Lee, ed., *Alternative Futures for Worship*, vol. 3, *The Eucharist* (Collegeville: The Liturgical Press, 1987) 21.

40. Michael A. Cowan, "Sacramental Moments: Appreciative Awareness in the Iron Cage," in Regis A. Duffy, ed., *Alternative Futures for Worship*, vol. 1, *General Introduction* (Collegeville: The Liturgical Press, 1987) 47.

41. John Naisbitt, *Megatrends: Ten New Directions Transforming Our Lives* (New York: Warner Books, 1984) 261. For a good study of modern patterns of marriage and its Christian models and symbols, see William J. Everett, *Blessed Be the Bond: Christian Perspectives on Marriage and Family* (Lanham, MD: University Press of America, 1990).

42. "The Plan of Pastoral Action for Family Ministry: A Vision and Strategy," *Origins* 15 (1985) 317.

43. *Familiaris Consortio* 17.

# 6

# Celebration of Love and Life: The Revised Roman Rite

IN A CONCLUSIVE STATEMENT AT THE END OF THE ROMAN SYNOD OF 1980, the bishops declared: "Everything we have said about marriage and family can be summed up in two words: love and life."[1] Because worship, love, and life should be intimately intertwined in a Christian marriage, the goal of any ritual expression should focus on the economy of salvation and its expression in contemporary human values. The revised Roman rite of marriage, approved in 1990 by Pope John Paul II, meets these goals.[2]

This chapter will study the general introduction, rites, and prayers of the new Order of Celebrating Marriage promulgated on 19 March 1990. Because this rite cannot be isolated from the former rite of 1969, especially in regard to structure and prayers, differences will be emphasized only in particular cases. The new rite will be analyzed in the light of: (1) its doctrinal background, new features, catechetical and formative components; (2) liturgical rationale and structure; (3) and the development of the liturgical celebration.

## LITURGICAL COMPONENTS

The importance of the celebration of the marriage passage has always been part of the Christian tradition. Unfortunately, the sacramentalization often failed to provide a fundamental direction for life and the grounding of a Christian identity, that is to say, a spirituality. There are many reasons for this failure. A major reason was the lack of a theology and spirituality based on the dynamic relationship between marriage and the biblical salvific story, centered in the nuptial reality of the "great mystery" of Christ and the new Christian community created by the Spirit. This is the central thread of meaning which the liturgy of marriage celebrates, but it was not clearly expressed in the pre-Vatican canonical models, including the austere rite in use till 1969.

*Background and New Features*

A celebration of love and life springing from the mystery of Christ, the archetypal model of marriage, was the goal of the first reform of the marriage rite promulgated in 1969. This reform constituted profound theological and pastoral renewal rooted in the sacramental theology of the mystery of salvation. Sacramental marriage was already seen as the continuation of the *historia salutis* which was actualized in the ritual celebration (*anamnesis*) and manifested in the life-long interpersonal covenant of the spouses.[3] Inaugurating a new sacramental and liturgical vision, this important symbolic, biblical, and textual enrichment of the first ritual reform opened up a new perception of the Catholic view of marriage; its more biblical and ecclesial, personalist and life-oriented dimensions were emphasized. Also the focus was on the concrete and wider realities of conjugal life.

The conciliar movement began to emphasize the nuptial meaning of the covenant, with all its implications in relation to the personal and communal commitments of married persons. The teaching of the Second Vatican Council's Constitutions on the Church, *Lumen Gentium*, and on the Church in the Modern World, *Gaudium and Spes*,[4] were incorporated into the introduction to the 1969 rite and inspired its texts and prayers. Nevertheless, further progress was made at the 1980 Synod on marriage and family life, in the ensuing apostolic exhortation of Pope John Paul II on the family and in the 1983 revised Code of Canon Law.[5] The second typical edition of the 1990 marriage rite was a liturgical response to various post-Vatican II doctrinal and ecclesiastical developments, which included a theology of the Christian family and new sacramental insights, especially the role of the Holy Spirit and the relationship of marriage to the sacraments of initiation, in which the "domestic church" is born and nourished.

Without any radical departure, as was the case with the previous reforms, the revised marriage rite builds upon the basic structure and themes of the previous one. In fact, the theological focus in both rites stems from the Christocentric and the historico-salvific view of marriage.[6] Their liturgy also sees the celebration of marriage as a total giving of mutual service, and a sacramental action which integrates every aspect of conjugal life and love. All these essential aspects converge into the same covenantal unity, Christology. These central themes as well as the new pastoral and liturgical insights of the 1969 reform not only remained in force, but were improved by the new 1990 version.

This new rite, which has to be translated into vernacular languages and adapted to different national cultures, has kept the same structure of the celebration.[7] Incorporating new insights of the post-conciliar reflection on marriage, the 1990 rite presents the sacrament as a sign of faith, a gift of the Holy Spirit, and a festive event of evangelization. The rite has been enriched in many ways. New prayers, some taken from ancient rituals, have been added. Prayers that are more biblical and more sensitive to modern culture, such as the idea of the equality and the complementarity of the spouses, are included. There are longer introductions to the rite, and these incorporate new theological and pastoral insights and emphasize the necessity of faith and the importance of adequate preparation. The biblical lectionary has been enlarged, and there are explicit references to the Holy Spirit in invoking the Spirit's grace upon the spouses within all the prayers of nuptial blessing.[8]

## Catechetical and Formative Components

With the expanded "introduction" (*Praenotanda*), the revised rite is a contemporary expression of the faith of the church in regard to sacramental marriage and an excellent pastoral instrument for marriage preparation. Although the catechetical and formative value of the rite depends on the entire process of preparation, celebration, and ongoing support of marriage, the introduction is an integral part of the entire articulation of the process of the marriage celebration. Together with the other sacramental moments of the Christian journey, this ritual celebration becomes a school of prayer and faith for the spouses. It is both a point of arrival and a point of departure in their Christian journey.

Although liturgy is primarily an action of praise and proclamation for God's mighty deeds in us, it is also catechetical in nature.[9] Its doctrinal source of inspiration is contained mainly in the prayer texts and in the scripture readings. In fact, the liturgical action is an experiential and transformative catechesis, because it is done in the context of prayer and proclamation. In teaching the spouses something concrete about the heart of their marriage journey, sacramental liturgy provides a foundational conjugal spirituality, namely, the central form of their freedom to love and to respond to God. But all this does not happen without adequate preparation. As in the case of other sacraments, "the sacrament of marriage presupposes and demands faith,"[10] which in turn requires formation before the celebration.

The introduction to the rite has four parts: dignity and importance of the sacrament; office and ministries in marriage preparation; actual preparation for the celebration; and the possibility of ritual adaptations by episcopal conferences. Following the instructional patterns common to all Roman liturgical books and rites as reformed and enriched after the Second Vatican Council, this general introduction contains the essential elements of the sacramental theology of marriage, of its catechesis and preparation, and explains the basic meaning of the structural elements of the rite.

We will now review the major themes that can be drawn from the introduction to the rite. These make the process of celebrating marriage a formative event at its best, as the ideals of marriage, expressed by the liturgical event, are accepted with living faith. Within a broad theological and catechetical view of the sacrament, three themes are prominent: (1) marriage is God's creative reality raised to the dignity of a *sacra-*

*ment,* (2) established as a *covenant* of intimate communion of life and love, (3) by which the spouses *signify and share* in the mystery of love and fidelity between Christ and the church.

First, marriage is seen in its divine source from which its goodness, unity, purpose, force, and strength are derived. The idea of a sacred and life-long bond, originating in God and effected by the irrevocable consent of the spouses, is stressed throughout. The sacramental nature of this bond is rooted in baptism, by which "a man and a woman are once for all brought into the covenant between Christ and the Church, so that their marital communion is assumed into Christ's own love and is enriched by the power of his sacrifice."[11]

From the paschal and covenantal mystery, marriage is related to the central sacraments that actualize this mystery, baptism and the eucharist. Hence the canonical implication with which the same paragraph ends: "Because of this new condition a valid marriage between the baptized is always a sacrament."

Second, this human bond makes an indissoluble covenant which images God's creating and redeeming relationship with us, and raised it to the sacramental dignity and holiness by the Bridegroom Jesus. It is a sign of the higher reality of the new covenant, as manifested in the wedding at Cana: "'As once God went to meet his people with a covenant of love and fidelity, so now the Saviour of the human race' offers himself as the bridegroom of the church, accomplishing the covenant with it in his paschal mystery."[12] In contrast with the contractual overemphasis of the past view of marriage, this view emphasizes that the essence of Christian marriage is spiritual, not legal.

This rooting in the history of salvation with its triple perspective (creation, prophets and Christ) of the divine-human love was provided by Vatican II, and remained with some improvements, the major view presented throughout the 1969 rite: a conjugal partnership "created out of love—sharing love—consecrated in love—destined to eternal love."[13]

Third, a sacramental marriage signifies and shares in the sacrificial and transformative, healing and fruitful mystery of grace by which Christ encounters the spouses. This is true not only of the liturgical celebration, but also of their married life: "Those who marry in Christ are empowered to celebrate effec-

tively with faith in God's word the mystery of Christ and the Church, to live rightly, and to bear witness in the eyes of all."[14]
This saving reality is God's gift and the Spirit's action:

> Through this sacrament the Holy Spirit brings it about that the spouses follow the example of Christ, who loved the church and gave himself for his bride. So too as Christian spouses they are to strive to nurture and foster their marriage in an equal dignity, with undivided love . . .[15]

Here the spirituality of conjugal life is seen in its paschal and pneumatic source. Married life and its purposes (mutual surrender, procreation, fruitful familial life and its mission) are integrated in the gift-bestowing love of God.

The theological, pastoral, and liturgical content of the introduction recaptures the best of western patristic tradition, is profound and basic, and is open to further doctrinal and catechetical improvements. It constitutes the heart of a celebration which should become the high point of a process of preparation and the initiation into an ongoing formation in marital, familial, ecclesial, and social spirituality. These future catechetical developments are the task of the national episcopal conferences, especially in regard to presenting other complementary models (like marriage as vocation) and to cultivating the necessary anthropological and cultural aspects of local churches.

## LITURGICAL FRAMEWORK

Love is a basic human experience which ordinarily culminates in the process of the incorporation of two committed persons into a new community of life. This new reality is filled with joy and expectations, tensions and promises. This new responsible partnership calls for ritual celebration. What is celebrated is more than the commitment of two persons, or the constitution of a family: human life itself is celebrated. It carries a promise for the future in the creative potential of love within all its personal and communal values. From the perspective of faith, this love is celebrated symbolically as the mysterious reality and sign of God's creative love and Christ's spirit to be lived out by the couple.

The essential theological content of this human and saving reality is found in biblical revelation and in the communal experience of people. Both demand the expression and actualization of the sacrament. Sacramental liturgy is, in fact, the best interpreter of the content of faith and human experience. It provides the spirituality needed by the challenging call to a liberating Christian discipleship in marriage. Thus, among all the varied social and ethnic customs that form the cultural context of the wedding rituals, the liturgy of marriage is the centerpiece. It is the action and event that can evoke the whole range of faith and experience, of values and emotions of a communitarian and festive celebration.

For a general understanding of and preparation for the celebration of a wedding liturgy, two topics of special importance have to be emphasized and will be approached first: rationale and structure.

*Liturgical Rationale*

Biblical symbolism provides the background and key to interpreting the specific and fundamental reason for the Christian celebration. This biblical symbolism expresses the outpouring of God's love, whose sign is the concrete conjugal life, and which culminates in the covenantal Christological and ecclesial mystery. Thus the pre-Vatican abstract and contractual conception of the "I ratify the bond of marriage you have contracted" of the Tridentine Roman Ritual (1614) was dropped. Instead the reformed rites (issued in 1969 and 1990) present a new articulation of consent in which the spouses, not the priest, are the protagonists, and the liturgical framework of the celebration centers on the reality of the biblical symbolism reenacted in the present conjugal bond.

Furthermore, the rite offers a concrete and existential vision of the vocation of the spouses, and ministers of the celebration, who "signify and participate" in the covenant of Christ.[16] Their celebration actualizes the presence of and the encounter with the total mystery of Christ. Symbols, words, and prayers focus on this mystery of graced love and call for its integration into "the intimate community of life and love."[17]

Grounded in Christ's mystery, this intimate community is

made holy in the sacrament of marriage by the presence and action of the Holy Spirit. As Armando Carideo says: "According to the biblical perspective, it is the Spirit of the risen Lord who 'effects' the dynamic relation between worship and life."[18] The Holy Spirit will remain the pledge of God's provident care in their marriage journey of inevitable human failures, of joys, trials, and triumphs. The liturgical reform brought about an awareness of the creative presence of the Spirit in the eucharistic and sacramental actions. As a consequence, the revised marriage rite (1990) takes into consideration the epiclectic (invocation of the Spirit's presence) dimension of the sacrament, especially in the formularies of nuptial blessing.[19] In fact, in the Spirit "the conjugal covenant instituted by the Creator" which already is "in a true and proper sense a journey toward salvation"[20] is completed by the celebration and living out of the sacrament "in spirit and in truth." Thus marriage constitutes a sacramental union of holiness empowered by the Spirit, "a true spiritual generation" in the words of John Chrysostom.[21]

*Liturgical Structure*

Ritually, two centers of the celebration are key to the rite's structure: the exchange of consent and the nuptial blessing. Love expressed in mutual consent is the root of the sacramental bond made possible by the spouses who acknowledge their calling from God before the community.

The nuptial blessing evokes God's salvific events exemplified by the saving reality of marriage. The biblical and theological themes presented in the prayers show the profound value of this blessing, as P.-M. Gy concludes:

> Nuptial fruitfulness and, in a broader sense, marriage are created and blessed by God; thus the blessing pronounced at the beginning remains for eternity. The Roman prayer adds to this fundamental theme to which the same idea of the blessing is linked, a development of the theme of the marriage of Christ and the church. It thus emphasizes the link between the creational blessing and the heart of the salvific mystery, the blessing accomplished in Christ's Easter.[22]

This blessing is placed within the eucharistic summit following the Lord's Prayer. According to tradition, the eucharistic covenant is the seal of the covenant of marriage.

From the perspective of ritual structure, a close study of the former Tridentine rite of marriage (referred to above), upon which the two post-conciliar rites depend, shows a polarization between the place of consent and the importance of the nuptial blessing. The result was an overly contractual view of the ritual and its sacramental meaning in disregard of its covenantal and anamnetic basis. Many past ambiguities in western tradition stem from such a polarization. The specific and essential elements of the rite, the role of the priest, and the structuring of the rite itself were unclear.

The origin of these ambiguities is historical. In fact, the nuptial blessing was the central element in the Roman marriage rite before the eleventh century. Nevertheless, the consent declared by the couple became not only an integral part of the ceremony after the eleventh century, but also the essential element of the sacrament according to the interpretation of scholastic theologians. The result was the ritual juxtaposition of cultural and juridical elements together with the sacramental and canonical.

Mutual consent and the nuptial blessing reveal the sacramental meaning of marriage and are the two principal moments on which the whole celebration hinges. They are a constant in the historical rituals of marriage during the eleventh and twelfth centuries, and they express the two essential aspects of its reality: the anthropological root of love manifested by the parties consent and the covenantal and eucharistic summit which seals the Christian character of marriage.

After the promulgation of the liturgical reform, the focus of the two Roman rites became more biblical and centered on the essential theme of covenant. This covenantal focus is central to the uniqueness and radical inner nature of the sacramental experience of Christian marriage. The salvific and paschal concept of the covenant of God with the people, and of Christ with the church, whose sign is the love of the spouses, provides the sacramental source of a concrete existential marriage spirituality. Thus the whole symbolism revolving around the concept of covenant becomes the radical sign of a Christian commitment and should be developed to its full potential in a ritual celebration as the archetypal mode of Christian marriage.

Some authors believe that the nuptial blessing should come immediately after the spouses' consent instead of the words of the priest receiving their consent, which represents a duplication.[23] This is what appears in the modern German ritual which places the nuptial blessing immediately after the rites of consent. However, the 1990 rite keeps intact the traditional structure.

Another important fact in regard to the liturgical structure of the ritual is the enrichment of creativity and inculturation. All Christian traditions have always included elements from local culture in their rites of marriage. In this regard, the revised rite is not a ritual-model, but rather a ritual-base from which the proper ritual has to be imaginatively adapted according to religious traditions, social customs, and the positive traits of the local culture.[24]

However, the consent of the spouses received by the presider and the nuptial blessing remain the two specific features of all Roman Catholic marriage rites.[25] Within the framework of the word of God and the eucharist, which are the prophetic voice and the heart of the mystery of marriage, there will always be the possibility of enriching the rites with new symbols and texts of national cultures.[26] These are the necessary means to the same goal of full participation in living out in faith and experiencing in love the human and divine "mysteria" celebrated.

The intrinsic link between worship and culture makes inculturation on the national marriage ritual an imperative, especially in non-western cultures. This complex language of symbols necessarily stems from the concrete world of beliefs and cultural creations. How can we develop a spirituality of marriage and basic values that is credible in contemporary society so that modern couples can rediscover their sense of identity? What rites do we need in order to safeguard the essential values of this always-new historical institution of marriage and the family, rites that help to overcome inevitable crises that make its purpose and meaning impossible?

By way of summary, we can broaden the liturgical framework and interpret the sacramentality of marriage by using the schema given in Figure 1, a schema depicting the three poles of marriage:

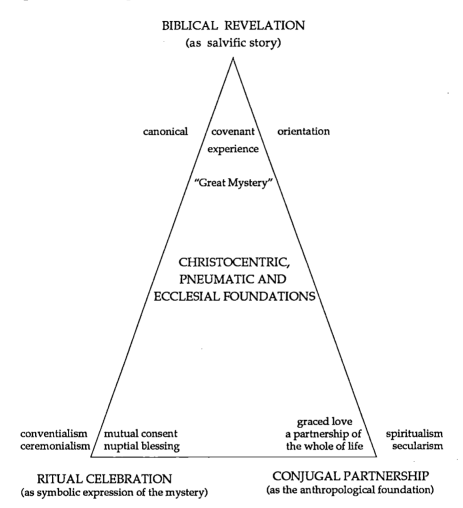

BIBLICAL  REVELATION
(as  salvific story)

canonical          covenant          orientation

experience

"Great Mystery"

CHRISTOCENTRIC,
PNEUMATIC AND
ECCLESIAL FOUNDATIONS

conventialism     mutual consent          graced love          spiritualism
ceremonialism     nuptial blessing        a partnership of     secularism
                                          the whole of life

RITUAL CELEBRATION                    CONJUGAL PARTNERSHIP
(as symbolic expression of the mystery)    (as the anthropological foundation)

(Figure 1)

A true celebration of faith and love depends on the valuing of each of these poles and on mutually integrating them in marriage: *biblical revelation* which becomes an actual salvific event; *conjugal partnership* which constitutes its sacramental root; and *ritual celebration* which is the salvific expression and actualization of its mystery of love and life. The inside words are key elements of the sacramental foundation and liturgical structure, while the external words, that is, conventionalism, ceremonialism, spiritualism, and secularism are some of the common deviations of sacramental praxis.

Wherever the canonical orientation prevails, it has to yield to a spirituality and praxis that manifests the economy of salvation. Bernard Haring has highlighted the need of this new orientation of a ministry of pastoral concern at the service of the married vocation. He writes:

> Above and beyond the question of the validity of the contracting of a sacramental marriage that has pushed itself into the foreground since the Council of Trent is the question of how the Church helps the believing Christian to be and to become an ever better effective sign of Christ's saving and healing love for spouse and children and milieu. Liturgical celebration and even the practice of the law are at the service of the vocation to become signs of salvation for and among each other.[27]

## THE LITURGICAL CELEBRATION

The new ritual order, liturgical compositions, and ministerial roles call for active and prayerful participation of the couple and the whole assembly in a truly communal and ecclesial celebration. But this will be an unrealistic objective without adequate planning for the celebration.[28] Planning and preparation are demanded, not only by the truthfulness of a sacrament of faith, especially since the couples are the ministerial protagonists of the ritual. They will not be "free" to participate fruitfully without some degree of maturity in their faith understanding of the ritual elements. A meaningful ritualization in a truly prayerful atmosphere should become a high point in the religious journey of the couple and the beginning of their conjugal spiritual life. In this case, liturgy becomes central, not only expressing the essential value of faith (*lex credendi*), but also being the paradigm for the spirituality of the conjugal beginning and formation.

As is true in all liturgical celebrations, the role of the presider in no less important, and this despite the theological fact that, "according to the ancient tradition, of the East and the West, it cannot be said that the intervention of the priest is per se essential to the sacramentality of marriage."[29] He makes possible a prayerful event which should also be a warm, festive, and solemn celebration.

Too often church weddings remain at the superficial and conventional level, ceremonious and pompous, but devoid of religious significance. The wedding event itself should be a celebration of freedom. As James L. Empereur points out, "the sacrament of marriage can either perpetuate the structures of society which lead to oppression or be a viable sign of the reality of God's justice and freedom in the world."[30] Marriage is, in fact, the sacrament of the consecration of two people to live out the covenant authentically. Rooted in the common traits of Christian living (personal prayer, eucharistic celebration, etc.) and not only concerned about mutual caring, this covenant spirituality should extend beyond the couple toward the common good and be open to the commitments of an ecclesial and social spirituality.

The liturgical celebration of the wedding is the climactic moment after the months of preparation for the engaged couple. The emphasis on the triple sacramental foundation of marriage (baptismal, celebrative, and eucharistic) is important for a vital celebration which, ideally, has three phases: the remote phase of preparation initiated with the primary foundation of baptism; the present phase of concrete actualization of the dignity and holiness of marriage in Christ; and the continuation phase of spiritual formation through the eucharist, "the source and climax of the Christian life" during the marriage journey. Needless to say, there are many other important human components involved in preparing for the vocation of marriage. Nevertheless, sacramental life, which must be extended to all aspects of life in a concrete way, is the core of the specific Christian call of the couple.

The second part of the introduction to the marriage rite[31] speaks about the ritual structure of the celebration. Its main elements are:

> liturgy of the word;
> consent of the contracting parties;
> nuptial blessing;
> eucharistic communion.

The place and importance of each element structuring the rite contribute to the rhythm of the celebration. The spouses are the protagonists of the action as the two high points of the liturgy indicate: the *exchange of consent* which takes place after the spiritual empowerment of the spouses by the word, and the *nuptial blessing* of their mutual covenant which is located in the eucharistic summit. Schematically, the entire celebration develops as indicated in Figure 2.

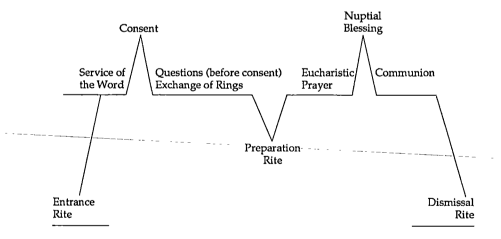

(Figure 2)

The following presentation of the elements of the celebration will not analyze all the details of the rite, but will make appropriate suggestions regarding its ritual content and meaning.

The *entrance rite* may take place at the door of the church, or at the place prepared for the couple. The first alternative is preferable. This flexibility allows for different arrangements of the entrance procession. An attitude of warmth that signals a gracious welcome, "showing that the church shares their joy,"[32] is very important and will create the right atmosphere for a joyful and prayerful celebration. This is confirmed by the introduction provided by the ritual. The introduction to the rite speaks of welcoming "with an open heart"[33] the spouses who should find in the liturgy the spiritual center of their lives.

Although the penitential rite is omitted, a rite of sprinkling with blessed water is appropriate, because this will provide a way of remembering the baptismal consecration. The opening prayer (there are six alternatives) concludes the gathering rite.

The *liturgy of the word* is an integral and essential part of the sacramental celebration. In fact, the gift of the word is a salvific event because it actualizes the mystery of the Bridegroom Jesus in the presence of the couple. The importance of God's word is obvious even when there is no eucharistic celebration; the word provides the salvation history context and the anamnetic element of the celebration.

The couple should be given an opportunity to select the readings (and other elements of the celebration) with the help of the minister; but they should not proclaim the Scriptures since the message of the readings is primarily addressed to them.

The *homily* should approach the biblical message as an announcement of faith and an expression of a joyful event, avoiding the extremes of moralism and polemics, as well as mysticism and lofty ideals unconnected with contemporary social realities. It should focus primarily on "the mystery of Christian marriage, the dignity of wedded love, the grace of the sacrament, and the responsibilities of married people, keeping in mind the circumstances of this particular marriage."[34]

The marriage celebration proper comprises four elements: the questions, the consent, the exchange of rings, and the nuptial blessing.

The preliminary *questions* do not repeat what was asked during the pre-nuptial investigation; rather, they are a public and liturgical proclamation of the conditions that make up a true Christian marriage: freedom of choice, lifelong faithfulness, and acceptance of children. This questioning of the parties leads to one of the two central elements of the rite, the consent, which together with the nuptial blessing is the essential element of the marriage rite.

The words of *consent* exchanged by the bridegroom and the bride is an ancient Anglo-Norman formula,[35] which has been adapted to meet modern reality. They express the indissolubility of marriage, as an irrevocable covenant of the mutual self-giving of the spouses. The Christian meaning of the joining of hands accompanying this exchange, expresses deeply the most fundamental reality of the union that blesses their lives: the mutual bond of love and fidelity. This formula, together with the other formulas of the ritualization of consent, corresponds in importance to the sacramental formulas of other rites, although in this case the declaration of consent has a more juridical character. Consequently, the presider should not change these formulas.

Immediately after the priest receives the couple's consent, he announces that they are married. The consent of the spouses forms their sacrament. The function of the priest in the reception of the consent is more than that of a "qualified witness of the church." He is a ministerial presider, a sign of the presence of Christ; by means of his blessing he ratifies the sacramental action accomplished by God through the couples covenant.

This new conception of the ministry of the presider is different from the ambiguous contractual mentality evoked by the pre-Vatican II formula of blessing pronounced by the priest, "ego coniungo vos . . ." Moreover, the new rite provides an alternative formula which appropriately emphasizes, in salvation history terms, the sacramental meaning of God's covenantal action. This action is symbolized by the couples bond of love which is assumed into Christ's own love. The new formula is: "May the God of Abraham, the God of Isaac, and the God of Jacob, the God who joined our first parents together in paradise, confirm and bless in Christ the consent you have expressed before the Church. What God has joined, no one must divide."[36]

The *blessing and exchange of rings* follow. Both gestures and formulas reaffirm the mutual union of love and fidelity already expressed by the consent. The meaning of the placing of a ring has a long evolution. It comes from the Roman custom at the time of engagement in which the bridegroom placed a ring on his bride's finger as a sign of personal possession. By the eleventh century some churches began to use two rings to signify the mutual giving of the parties in perpetual fidelity. This custom made its way into the Roman Ritual of 1614.[37]

The priest blesses the rings and gives them to the spouses. First, the husband places his wife's ring on her ring finger, and the wife places her husband's ring on his finger. At the same time, they may recite a brief formula which is very ancient and meaningful: "N., take this ring as a sign of my love and fidelity . . ." It is very fitting for the assembly to respond with a song of praise or a joyful liturgical hymn.[38] As in the case of the acclamation after the exchange of consent, the ritual should be enriched by the active participation of the celebrating assembly through responses, acclamations, and song.

The general intercessions conclude the liturgy of the word and this first part of the marriage rite. Spontaneous petitions, not limited to the married people, could be added by the participants.

The *eucharistic liturgy* is the proper way to celebrate marriage since both realities are intimately connected:

> The eucharist is the very source of Christian marriage . . . In this sacrifice of the New and Eternal Covenant Christian spouses encounter the source from which their own marriage covenant flows, is interiorly structured and continuously renewed.[39]

The spouses are invited to carry the eucharistic gifts to the altar and to share in the eucharistic bread and cup. The parents of the couple could be invited to join them in presenting the gifts. Particularly rich in theological content, the various preface formulas are a centerpiece in the covenantal proclamation of the spouses' love. The third preface beautifully expresses the mystery of love: "Love is man's origin, love is his constant calling, love is his fulfillment in heaven. The love of man and woman is made holy in the sacrament of marriage, and becomes the mirror of your everlasting love."[40]

The first three eucharistic prayers use various formulas to pray for the spouses who are mentioned by name. Thus the spouses continue to be at the center of the church at prayer through the eucharistic action, and are led to new depths of participation in the highest expression of their own "spiritual sacrifice."[41] But realistically all this fruitful participation is only possible with adequate preparation, and should be carried on in a concrete eucharistic and Christocentric spirituality reflecting the realities proper to their married life.

The marriage rite climaxes with the consecratory prayer of the *nuptial blessing*. Following the ancient Roman tradition already attested in the Gelasian Sacramentary (seventh-eighth centuries), this prayer is proclaimed after the Lord's Prayer and stresses the eucharistic meaning of marriage: "that through the sacrament of the body and blood of Christ, he will unite in love the couple he has joined in this holy bond."[42] The rite demands a moment of reverent silence before the priest's blessing as an effective way of contemplative preparation.

Found in all Christian liturgies of marriage, the nuptial blessing is the original element of the Christian celebration of marriage. Already documented in the fourth century at Rome and in the Eastern Churches, it became the normative prayer for the solemn blessing of marriage, and was already made compulsory during the ninth-tenth centuries for the marriage of clergy.[43]

The rite offers several alternative formulas, which have been especially revised to include an explicit invocation of the Spirit's action upon the spouses: "Send upon them the grace of the Holy Spirit, so that, with our love in their hearts, they may remain faithful in the marriage covenant."[44] They generally develop the biblical themes of salvation history, and their structure corresponds to the consecratory preface of priestly ordination. They are anamnetic and epiclectic prayers proclaiming the sacramental dimension of the love of the spouses as grounded in God's creative purpose and in God's covenant with humanity accomplished in the nuptial mystery of the Lord's Pasch. This relationship between God's foundational mystery and its expression in married life is one of the most frequent themes; for example, the second nuptial blessing requests that the spouses "as they begin to live this sacrament . . . may share with each other the gifts of your love and become one in heart and mind as witness to your presence in their marriage."[45]

The symbolic action in which the core meaning of marriage and eucharist intersect is the couple's sharing in the Lord's eucharistic body and blood—the nuptial banquet of Christ's love. Both marriage and eucharist are sacraments of love: the former, as specific sign, flowing from the latter, the total sign of the mystery. The prayers after communion should emphasize this vital relationship by expressing its central aspects in a meaningful manner.

The *solemn blessing* of the concluding rite is a threefold blessing adopted from the ancient Gallican and Hispanic marriage liturgies. The formulas are varied and profound. The first blessing, incisive and pastoral, gives the newlyweds a summary of an ideal matrimonial life in its concrete realities, its mission, and its fruits and blessings:

* God the eternal Father keep you in love with each other, so that the peace of Christ may stay with you and be always in your home.

* May your children bless you, your friends console you and all men live in peace with you.

* May you always bear witness to the love of God in this world so that the afflicted and the needy will find in you generous friends, and welcome you into the joys of heaven.[46]

*Order for Celebrating Marriage Outside Mass.* When the liturgy of the eucharist is not celebrated, the marriage rite continues, after the general intercessions, with the Lord's Prayer and the nuptial blessing; it ends with the concluding rite. Communion may be distributed from the reserved sacrament. In this case, the Our Father is recited before communion.

A deacon may preside at this rite. Moreover, it is now allowed for the marriage to be celebrated before an assisting layperson; a complete Order with proper texts is provided for this purpose.[47] In such cases the relationship between marriage and the eucharist is weakened; as Kenneth Stevenson observes: "a deacon may solemnize this kind of marriage, which, though pastorally needful in some areas, is hardly theologically appropriate and serves to make this form of the rite even more second class."[48] Another type of Order is provided for a non-eucharistic marriage with a catechumen or non-Christian. The ritual structure for celebrating marriage outside Mass is followed, but the third nuptial blessing is used.[49]

## Notes

1. "A Message to Christian Families in the Modern World," *Origins* 10 (1980) 325.

2. *Ordo Celebrandi Matrimonium, Editio Typica Altera,* (3-19-1990). I am very grateful to the International Commission on English in the Liturgy, Inc. (ICEL) in Washington, D.C., which allowed me to use its English translation (draft form) of the rite.

3. See these selected articles on the 1969 marriage rite: P.-M. Gy, "Le nouveau rituel romain du mariage," *La Maison-Dieu* 99 (1969) 125-143; F. Brovelli, "La celebrazzione del matrimonio," *Rivista Liturgica* 4 (1976) 500-528; Th. Maas-Ewerd, "Zur liturgishen Feier der Trauung," *Lebendige Seelsorge* 3/4 (1977) 186-191; Kenneth W. Stevenson's book, to be cited in footnote 26, also studies the rite, pp. 124-230.

4. Especially the following articles: *Lumen Gentium* 11, 35, 41 and *Gaudium et Spes* 12, 47-52, 61; see also the Constitution on the Sacred Liturgy 77.

5. The Apostolic Exhortation on the Family (*Familiaris Consortio*) by John Paul II (11-22-1981), especially nos. 13 and 51. The *Code of Canon Law* (1983), Title VII. The sacramental experience and theology of the post-Vatican II reform also contributed to the enrichment of the new marriage rite.

6. See Achile M. Triacca, "La 'celebrazione' del matrimonio. Aspetti teologico-liturgici. Contributo alla spiritualita sacramentaria e alla pastorale liturgica," Piannazzi in *Realta e valore del sacramento del matrimonio* (Rome: LAS, 1976) 103-152.

7. For the official promulgation and introduction (*praenotanda*), see *Notitiae* 287 (1990) 301-327; also Luca Brandolini, "La pastorale del matrimonio," *Notitiae* 288 (1990) 357-364; Achile M. Triacca, "Spiritus Sancti Virtutis Infusio: A proposito di alcune tematiche teologico-liturgiche testimoniate nell' 'Editio Altera' dell' 'Ordo Celebrandi Matrimonium'," *Notitiae* 26 (1990) 365-390.

8. Among the new elements, the 1990 rite has: a new introduction of forty-four paragraphs (the 1969 rite had only eighteen); two additional opening prayers taken from the Verona and Gelasian Sacramentaries; revised prayers for the nuptial blessing; an increase in the number of these prayers, from three to five; and five new biblical readings; see this new study, José M. Rodríguez, "Nueva Edición del Ritual del Matrimonio: Teología y Pastoral," *Phase* 187 (1992) 13-26.

9. For this reason, a special chapter of this book is devoted to the exploration of the biblico-liturgical theology of marriage celebration.

10. *Ordo Celebrandi* 16.

11. Ibid. 7; see 1 and 4.

12. Ibid. 6; see 2 and 5.

13. Dionisio Borobio, "Matrimonio," in Dionisio Borobio and others, *La Celebración en la Iglesia: Sacramentos* (Salamanca: Sígueme, 1988) 541.

14. *Ordo Celebrandi* 11; see 6.

15. Ibid. 9.

16. Ibid. 8; see Eph 5:25.

17. Ibid. 4.

18. Armando Carideo, *La celebrazione del matrimonio Cristiano* (Bologna: Edizioni Dehoniane, 1977) 193.

19. The new rite has five prayers for the nuptial blessing in which explicit epiclectic references are introduced; see *Notitiae* 287 (1990) 301-317.

20. *Familiaris Consortio* 68; *Origins* 11 (1981) 459.

21. *Homily* 20, 5 (PG 62:135).

22. Gy, "Le nouveau rituel" 137.

23. See Herman Schmidt, "Rituals and Sacramentality of Christian Marriage," *Questions liturgiques et paroissiales* 56 (1975) 38; also Gy, "Le nouveau rituel" 136.

24. See *Ordo Celebrandi* 39-44. For example, the traditional "crowning of the bride or the veiling of bride and groom may be added" (ibid. 41).

25. They must always be present (ibid. 42).

26. A greater freedom than in the case of other sacraments is given in regard to the preparation of national rituals, so that "each conference of bishops may draw up its own marriage rite" (ibid. 42). Anscar J. Chupungco speaks of five ways of accomplishing this: *Liturgies of the Future: The Process and Methods of Inculturation* (New York: Paulist Press, 1989) 139-149. Two other resources books are: Kenneth W. Stevenson, *To Join Together: The Rite of Marriage* (New York: Pueblo, 1987) esp. 187-210; Bernard Cook, *Alternative Futures for Worship: Christian Marriage* (Collegeville: The Liturgical Press) 1987.

27. Bernard Haring, *No Way Out: Pastoral Care of the Divorced and Remarried* (Middlegreen [England]: St. Paul Publications, 1990) 33-34.

28. An example of a practical resource is Paul Covino, ed., *Celebrating Marriage: Preparing the Wedding Liturgy, A Handbook For Engaged Couples* (Washington, D.C.: The Pastoral Press, 1987).

29. Gy, "Le nouveau rituel" 134. Following Duns Scotus, Pius XII in his encyclical *Mystici Corporis* already affirmed that "the spouses are ministers of grace to themselves" (AAS 35 [1943] 202).

30. "Marriage: A Liberating Relationship," in James L. Empereur and Christopher G. Kiesling, *The Liturgy That Does Justice* (Collegeville: The Liturgical Press, 1990) 200; see also Christopher G. Kiesling, "The Liturgy of Christian Marriage: Introduction to Marital Spirituality," *Spirituality Today* 34 (1982) 48-59.

31. *Ordo Celebrandi* 35.

32. Ibid. 45.

33. Ibid. 53.

34. Ibid. 57.

35. See *Manuale ad Usum Percelebris Ecclesiae Sarisburiensis* (Salisbury), ed. A.J. Collins (London, 1960) 47-48. The joining of hands, an important constant of the western and Christian cultures, was adopted from the ancient custom whereby authority was transferred from the father to the husband.

36. *Ordo Celebrandi* 64.

37. See Adolf Adam, *Foundations of Liturgy: An Introduction to Its History and Practice* (Collegeville: The Liturgical Press, 1992) 236.

38. *Ordo Celebrandi* 68.

39. *Familiaris Consortio* 57.

40. *Ordo Celebrandi* 236.

41. *Familiaris Consortio* 56.

42. *Ordo Celebrandi* 73.

43. K. Ritzer, *Le Mariage dans les églises chrétiennes du Ier au XIe siècle* (Paris: Editions du Cerf, 1970) 104-123.

44. *Ordo Celebrandi* 74.

45. Ibid.

46. Ibid. 77.

47. Ibid. 121-151.

48. Stevenson, *To Join Together* 142.

49. *Ordo Celebrandi* 172.

# 7

# Marriage as Covenant: A Biblico-Liturgical Theology

MARRIAGE IS THE SACRAMENTAL COVENANT. WHEN A MAN AND A woman have grown in love, they unite in an intimate bond, which is called covenant. Vatican II says:

> The intimate partnership of married life and love has been established by the Creator and qualified by His laws. It is rooted in the conjugal covenant of irrevocable personal consent.[1]

Covenant, as a graced and intimate personal encounter between God and people fulfilled in Christ, is a major referent of Christian sacramentality, and in particular the sacramentality of marriage. Moreover, the biblical concept of covenant provides an integrated vision of a concrete and existential marriage spirituality evoked in the wedding liturgy.

The living sign of marriage proclaims the silent mystery of God. Marriage is itself a natural sign which speaks of love and fidelity. The Christian symbolism of marriage derives from this anthropological reality, which mediates God's presence, and thus provides in biblical revelation a more personal and intimate vision of the loving and faithful God. Marriage is a sign of God's presence and metaphor for God's love. In fact, marriage becomes a privileged sign of God's re-creating presence in our world. Again, Vatican II: "Authentic married love is caught up into divine love and is governed and enriched by Christ's redeeming power and the saving activity of the Church."[2] As part of God's plan, marriage is the work of grace, and consequently requires the ritual and ecclesial celebration by which God's love is actualized in the life of the couple. The church's wedding is the privileged and symbolic expression of the real presence of the bridegroom Jesus in the everyday lives of the spouses.

Elaborating on this covenantal vision, the 1980 International Synod in Rome proposed a family and marriage spirituality stemming from a theology according to "God's plan for marriage and the family."[3] It is a theology based on a salvific concept of marriage found in the spirituality of creation, the covenant, the cross, the resurrection, and the new community. This is the theological framework which guides the following reflection on the biblico-liturgical content of the liturgy of marriage. In fact, sacramental liturgy centers on the great mysteries of the economy of salvation in the love and the life experienced by the spouses.

Marriage is a stage of human existence which is in itself a salvific reality. Consequently, it is expressed and accomplished in the ritual celebration and the living out of the mystery of Christ. The sacramentalization of marriage, beginning with the wedding and festivities, initiates a salvific story of the new life journey and being of the spouses: their mutual social responsibility and commitment to the community of the Spirit who dwells in their hearts.

Remembrance (*anamnesis*) is a key element at the heart of the sacramentality of marriage. In the rite of marriage we remember the presence and action of Christ's Spirit in our midst, doing so within the broad view of the salvation history experience of God's people in biblical revelation. This recalling of the history of salvation is presented in the rite through the rich tapestry of biblical readings, prayers and other symbols. Biblico-liturgical theology is drawn from the rite, as we will do in this chapter. Theology, catechesis, and the spirituality of marriage all draw significance from salvation history and from the anthropological relevance of the created reality of marriage (God's creation). It leads to its Christocentric foundation (God's redemption). In the wedding liturgy God's deeds and the story of Jesus as related to the couple are remembered and proclaimed with faith and obedience.

The marriage liturgy, incorporating God's plan of salvation history, relates the vision of the couple's partnership to the couple's ecclesial vocation of Christian identity and mission. The proclamation of God's gifts and future hopes is centered within the consecration of their love and life vocation. Furthermore, this biblico-liturgical remembrance has an educative and formative function within the domestic church, "helping its members to become agents of the history of salvation and living signs of God's loving plan for the world."[4] Liturgical spirituality and conjugal life form a vital synthesis which is integral to the life-journey of the Christian family.

In the historical proclamation of the liturgy, Scripture becomes the living word of God's self-communication to the couple. Thus, liturgy is an essential source and expression of the theology of marriage. This biblico-liturgical theology establishes a marital foundation for a family spirituality based on faith and love (see 1 Jn 4:7-21). This foundation is rooted in the spirituality of creation, the covenant, the resurrection, and the new community. These are the themes we will now discuss, using as a principal basis the prayers and scriptural texts found in the rituals of marriage in both east and west.

## SIGN OF THE MYSTERY OF CREATION

The spouses are God's co-creators of the gift of life (procreation) and of the new and first experience of love. They build community and make history through their commitment to themselves and society.[5]

The created reality of marriage is a major theme of the marriage liturgy where it is presented not simply as an historical fact but in relation to the "great mystery" (Eph 5:32). This mystery has been described as "the very reality of salvation in its entirety, the reality within which Christian marriage is located, from which it emerges and which it also brings to expression."[6] As created reality, marriage has a direct relationship to the divine source evoked and actualized by the liturgical remembrance in the light of the Christological and ecclesial mystery.

The marriage liturgy presents us with a basic and broad mystagogy or introduction into the mystery of essential biblical and Christian beliefs: marriage is the fruit of God's creative love, and each spouse becomes God's own partner destined to cooperate in the divine plan of creation, within the relationship of the intimate and permanent conjugal union. All these beliefs are integrated in the economy of salvation celebrated by the sacrament. The essential perspective of the liturgical prayers is Trinitarian and Christocentric. Thus the Triune presence of the creative and redemptive source of marriage is seen in the act of creation and is realized also in the sacramental action. The celebration of the covenant makes possible this salvation history perspective because a fundamental relationship exists between God, creator and savior, and God's covenant with humanity as manifested, according to Schillebeeckx, in the marital relationship.[7]

Personal and communal, realistic and passionate, respectful of individual equality and dignity, fragile and yet strong as death (Song 8:6), the mystery of conjugal union and love can never be exhausted. In the light of the mystery of Christ a contemporary interpretation is also needed. Genesis provides, in fact, an archetypal parable of the meaning of human life and love together with the inspiration for a critical anthropology. The major themes of Genesis in this regard are: love between a man and a woman is *a mystery of loneliness and encounter* (Gn 2:20), of *equality and mutual attraction* (Gn 2:21-24), of *enigma and revelation* (Gn 2:21), and of *harmony and vulnerability* (Gn 2:25; 3:7).[8]

*The Lutheran Book of Worship* offers an excellent example of Christian realism inspired by God's creative plan for humanity, and of unfailing hope and source of fortitude for the spouses in facing the lifetime vicissitudes of the marriage journey:

> The Lord God in his goodness created us male and female, and by the gift of marriage founded human community in a joy that begins now and is brought to perfection in the life to come.
>
> Because of sin, our age-old rebellion, the gladness of marriage can be overcast and the gift of the family can become a burden.
>
> But because God, who established marriage, continues still

to bless it with his abundant and ever-present support, we can be sustained in our weariness and have our joy restored.[9]

The 1990 Roman rite of marriage well reflects the contemporary search for a balanced view of the human realities, especially as to the role of the spouses within marriage and the meaning of a human love that is not idealized. The personalist view of the marital encounter is balanced with marriage's social implications and ministerial vocation.

In this regard, Francis Schüssler Fiorenza has emphasized the importance of this relationship to the community in our society. He points out that a relationship is developed

> as a community of intersecting relationships and interests. In the love of spouses for one another, all these elements are intermingled: friendship and passion, desire and generosity, communality and individuality, personal and communal interests. One does not pass from one to the other as if a stage of eros leads to a stage of agape, as if desire leads to solidarity, or friendship leads to love. Instead, love, friendship, inclusion of others, and the intersecting of diverse and common interests coexist each strengthening one another."[10]

## SIGN OF THE MYSTERY OF THE COVENANT

Covenant defines the relationship between God and his people and ultimately between God and all humanity. Creation is the first covenantal act of God who is the life-giver, the liberator, the lord of history. The unconditional covenant God made with Abraham became the liberating, sacrificial covenant of Sinai. God liberates and calls all to holiness (Ex 19:4-6), establishing a bond based on the divine word and its acceptance by the people, and sealed by a sacrificial ritual (Ex 24:1-11). The Sinai covenant marks the beginning of a new creation in which the priestly people are led to communion with God.

Both Hebrew traditions, the Yahwist which presents the communion meal before God and the Elohist which refers to the sprinkling with blood, stress the same profound meaning: the sharing of life and intimacy in a family relationship, or spiritual consanguinity between God and the people. The father-son and husband-wife relationship is clearly stated in the prophetic description of the re-creation and renewal by the spirit of God in the messianic age: "I will be their God and they shall be my people" (Jer 31:33). This covenant establishes a personal relationship characterized by love, fidelity, and devotion, as imaged by the marriage relationship in the vision of Hosea, Jeremiah, and other prophets.[11]

The mystery of the new covenant with humanity is manifested in God's self-gift to humanity in Christ. The imagery of life-giving, encounter, sacrificial wedding, and total communion describes in unsurpassable ways the covenant themes in the New Testament.[12]

Marriage is also covenant in its core. The intrinsic relationship between covenant and marriage has, therefore, a salvation history basis in a double sense: symbolic and paradigmatic. The symbolic language of marriage opens up a new dimension of the reality of God. By God's action people come closer to God and are introduced into the divine mystery. Marriage is part of God's transcendent mystery. Also, the biblical covenant represents a spiritual paradigm of the interpersonal and communal realities of marriage.

Marriage, however, has its own ambiguities. God and Israel were unequal partners. Furthermore, the superior status of man and the inferior status of woman in Hebrew society is derived from a misunderstanding of the covenant. This concept has led some to conclude that marriage is not "an image of the covenantal relationship between God and Israel, as symbolized in the prophetic literature."[13] Similar reservations have been based on the classical text from Ephesians (Eph 5:21-33) which presents the Christ-church relationship as a paradigm of the husband-wife partnership. The symbolism "places the husband in the role of ruler and savior and the wife in the role of sinner and subordinate."[14]

The life-creating and salvific message of the covenant certainly becomes relevant when this message responds to contemporary religious consciousness. Sensitive as they are to the egalitarian patterns in marriage in western culture, these reservations reflect, however, a narrow religious interpretation of the texts. There is certainly a danger of mechanistic interpretations which seek to substantiate an anachronistic status of women with an isolated text. Besides, the need of a critical stance in tune with the demands of the present, a faith interpretation of the covenant, must, above all, touch the heart of its message and must make it a spring of meaning for today. This covenant has to be put into practice in its ethical demands and in a new spirit of marital relations.

In fact, inequality and subservience of the woman were not intended by the first covenant of God in creation; and yet these were seen by the Hebrew authors to be a result of human sin.[15] It is the couple's embodied faith that makes them a people of the covenant, that makes their union a sign of the covenant. Celebrated in word and symbol in the marriage liturgy as well as in the eucharist, this covenant actualizes the prototype of all covenants, namely, Christ's. Thus the mystery of conversion to radical equality and dignity should characterize the commitment to a shared life in matrimony.

Liturgy makes possible this creative fidelity to Scripture and also establishes a creative link between the celebration of marriage and Christian praxis in a concrete cultural reality. Whereas in the past the language and certain symbolic actions of the ritual reflected sex roles of subordination,[16] less personalist meanings of the relationship, and a more individualist spirituality, today's rituals and doctrine should convey a relevant spirituality which is more attentive to the human and social values of modern marriage: personal equality and social consciousness, a commitment to the inner community of life-creating and caring, and a commitment to the church's mission of service.

Both western and eastern marriage rituals have too few significant references to marriage as a prophetic image of God's covenant with the people. The purpose of these references is to illustrate God's absolute and everlasting fidelity as opposed to the unpredictable and fallible, yet intentionally irrevocable personal consent of the spouses. This personal consent does not depend on a juridical concept of the mutual self-giving. It also includes affective and vital components. The marriage covenant should reveal the actualization of God's covenant: "Father, to reveal the plan of your love you made the union of husband and wife an image of the covenant between you and your people."[17]

The nuptial blessing of the marriage rite (1969) was inspired by the theology of the conciliar doctrine: "Just as of old God encountered his people with a covenant of love and fidelity, so our savior, the spouse of the church, now encounters Christian spouses through the sacrament of marriage."[18] This mysterious encounter does not disclose simply an ideal to be followed or a goal to be obtained in conjugal life. This life is a sign of God's revealed mystery in word and eucharist, a mystery that discloses the origin and total reality of conjugal life. As Joseph A. Selling points out:

> It should be stressed that the love which the wife has for her husband is modeled on the love of Christ for his church equally as is the love of husband for his wife, a love of "perpetual fidelity through mutual self-bestowal." When this occurs and only when this occurs, can we speak of sacrament in the Christian sense.[19]

The celebration of marriage is anamnetic, that is, its function is to express the reality of God's saving presence and grace in the midst of the covenant experience of the spouses' journey as this experience evokes the history of salvation. This is the theme of many of the nuptial prayers. God is present: "The witness to these words (of consent) is the God who is enthroned invisibly above this altar."[20] God is also the author and guide of today's marriage just as was true in biblical history:

> O Lord our God, you have sent forth your truth upon your inheritance, and your covenant unto your servants, our fathers, your elect from generation to generation; Look upon your servant, N., and your handmaiden, N, and confirm their betrothal in faith, oneness of mind, fidelity and love."[21]

## SIGN OF THE CROSS AND RESURRECTION

The marriage metaphor for God's covenant likewise becomes a symbol of Christ's nuptial relationship to his church. Marriage manifests the redemptive mission of Christ in the church. Sacramental marriages share in the reality of grace through these expressions of God's presence, fully realized in Jesus Christ, and made alive in the total self-giving of the spouses. The reality of the cross is a sign of Christ who in the "perfect love" of his Pasch (Jn 13:1) became the living example and prototype of the spouses' new way of life. Thus the paradoxical death and resurrection of Jesus is realized in marriage when the spouses follow in freedom and fidelity the new way of the cross, based not on the perfection of the law, but on the perfection of compassion: "Be perfect (compassionate) just as your Father is perfect" (compassionate) (see Mt 5:48; Lk 6:36).

### The Christ Event Grounds the Sacramental Covenant

In restoring marriage not only to its original design (Mt 19:4-9) but also relating it to his salvific work, Jesus gives marriage its ultimate meaning. Those who follow him make present the kingdom yet to come and carry out the presence of its reality and values. In fact, Jesus uses the language of the nuptial experience to communicate the realities of his kingdom, like mystery, joy, and vigilance.[22] This is so because marriage contains and calls for the values that characterize the kingdom: peace, justice, solidarity, and joyful hope.

Christ's mystery of the total and permanent espousal of the church is fully consummated in his love unto death on the cross for his bride. "In reality, the mystery of Christ which realized the redemption of men is a nuptial mystery, where God and humanity meet face to face as husband and wife."[23]

John's narrative of the wedding at Cana (Jn 2:1-11) has to be read in the light of that mystery since the narrative contains a symbolic meaning of the paschal and eucharistic realization expressed in marriage. Jesus is the new bridegroom who offers (in the water jars of the old covenant) the new wine of the messianic wedding covenant and thus reveals his glory. In Jesus' hour (his glorified cross) Mary is present as the church-bride figure and co-protagonist. This event is a prophetic manifestation of the reality of the Christ-church's wedding sealed by the self-surrender of the cross.

In the rituals of marriage the reading of the Canaan wedding is often introduced by a reference to a text on marriage in Ephesians (5:25; 32) that focuses on its symbolic-sacramental meaning. "The Canaan wedding is thus a foretaste of the messianic banquet, as the celebration of the Christian spouses is the sign and realization of a transcendent reality."[24] Husband and wife are offered a family spirituality as they read God's word in the context of their own personal and social experience.

The classic text of a Christocentric view of marriage is Ephesians 5:21-33. This text establishes the sacramental source of the conjugal community: "This is a great mystery; but I am saying it applies to Christ and the church" (Eph 5:32). The "great mystery" refers to the triple relationship of the spousal mystery: (1) hidden in the Adam-Eve typological figuration (Gn 2:24); (2) revealed in the salvific relationship of Christ-church and, (3) signified in the reciprocal husband-wife communion. This prophecy is a pre-figuration of an ideal conjugal society before the fall which was reconstituted in the paradigmatic model for husband and wife in the paschal sacrifice of the eternal bridegroom. Christ is the total reality of the "two in one flesh," joined in oblatory love: "Just as Christ loved the church and sacrificed himself for her to make her holy. He made her clean by washing her with a form of words" (Eph 5:25-26—bath of baptism).

This mystery grounds the realities and qualities needed in a genuine yet always imperfect Christian community. The community is already initiated into the paschal sacrifice by the great sacrament (Christian initiation). Marriage seals the relationship of faith and commitment of the two spouses and is in itself an appropriate image of the meaning of Christian initiation. JoAnn Heaney-Hunter points out this analogy from her reading of John Chrysostom:

> In the *First Baptism Instruction* Chrysostom establishes the links between Christian marriage and Christian initiation by declaring that in both, individuals make total commitments: the spouses to each other, and the neophyte to God. He points out that even Paul is amazed by the strength of the bond that exists in a married couple. His nuptial imagery provides a concrete example for the entire Christian community: the depth and breath of initiatory commitment similar to the depth and breath of commitment found in the best Christian marriages.[25]

As qualified partners in the covenant of the cross, the spouses will always need a concrete actualization of their faith in a never-ending process of becoming partners with Christ. Christian marriage thus exemplifies the realized potential of God's original covenant with humanity.

Speaking from the perspective of God's presence and action in creation, Karl Rahner is decisive in regard to the salvific dynamics of marriage: the personal and unifying love of self-surrender that creates the state of marriage has its fundamental reason and absolute goal in God who sustains it by divine grace. This reality of salvation is manifested in the unity between Christ and the church. This unity effects the full manifestation of the bond of marriage because both are in fact internally related. Thus, Rahner affirms: "The unity between Christ and the church is the ultimate cause and origin of the unity of marriage."[26] The "great mystery" is the foundation of the marriage sacrament which shares in Christ's redeeming work in the faith and self-giving love of the spouses. Marriage, like all sacraments, receives its transforming power from the source of the paschal event. Concretizing this spiritual power in their own proper path of life, spouses find here the archetype of their marital spirituality.

Christ's cross and resurrection establish not only the new mode of existence for every Christian but also the particular graced relationship for every marriage and family. This Easter faith is the center from which to consider the Pauline mandate to "marry in the Lord." This is true since the early Christian communities saw their corporate existence as drawing meaning from the focus of the Christological mysteries.

This new mode of being and living in Christ emerges from the personal and cosmic restoration accomplished by the resurrection: "Lead a life worthy of your vocation. Bear with one another in love . . ." (Eph 4:1-2). Empowering the person to receive God's grace allows the other to begin a "new life in the Spirit." This calls for a permanent attitude of conversion to acceptance, fidelity, joy, reconciliation; an attitude of new beginnings, a reaching out to those in need, and other aspects of a liberating spirituality rooted in the paschal mystery. Vatican II stated this vocation meaningfully:

> In the footsteps of Christ, the principle of life, they will bear witness by their faithful love in the joys and sacrifices of their calling, to that mystery of love which the Lord revealed to the world by his death and resurrection.[27]

*Sacramental Spirituality: Nurturing Center for the Family*

Sacramental spirituality empowers Christians and shapes

them to a life-style that is consistent with their Christian vocation. This spirituality can neither be limited to the day the
marriage is solemnized, nor can it be reduced to the living out
of the baptismal faith. Baptismal faith has to be made concrete
through the qualities that enable the complex relationship of
marriage and family life to pursue their own unique path to
holiness. Nevertheless, the essential features of Christian and
marital spirituality will always be found in the sacramental
center. Moreover, there are parallels between spirituality in
general and the virtues that integrate a contemporary spirituality of married love. "A marriage matures as a direct result
of these same choices about life-style, career, relationship and
resources."[28]

The nuptial and symbolic mystery that joins Christ and the
church is one of the major themes of the reformed Roman liturgy of marriage. Marriage is not only one of the clearest symbols of what God is, but it is also the anamnetic sign of
Christ's mystical body. This theology is especially expressed
in the nuptial blessing of the spouses: "Father, you have made
the union of man and wife so holy a mystery, that it symbolizes the marriage of Christ and his church."[29]

The eastern liturgies are far more eloquent in their mystical
and profoundly spiritual view of marriage. The intimate connection and dependence among the nuptial, paschal, and eucharistic mysteries flow from the Christ-church covenantal
theme, as in the following examples of the Maronite liturgy:

> May the Lord Jesus Christ, spouse of justice and truth, who has
> betrothed the church of nations and has forged with his blood a
> ring with the nails of crucifixion . . . Now, Lord, may this ring
> that is given to our son, N., and to our daughter, N., be like the
> mystical ring with which the daughter of nations has been mar-
> ried, the one who received the body and blood for the pardon
> of faults and forgiveness of sins."[30]

> O Christ, the bridegroom, you betrothed the holy and faithful
> church; in the upper room you gave her your body and blood
> and sealed your nuptial covenant with her."[31]

Christian tradition has always considered the eucharist as
the generative center of marriage and family spirituality because, as Karl Rahner says, the eucharist "is the sacrament of

the heart of Christ" and consequently, "the source of our love for our brothers and sisters."[32]

This applies especially to marriage, the natural place where the eucharist is the ultimate conclusion and manifestation of the caring love of Christ. The participation in the eucharist incorporates the spouses into that mystery of the living Christ.

What Augustine affirms concerning the intrinsic relationship between the eucharist and the ecclesial body has a meaningful application to partnership with the domestic church: "Your own mystery is placed on the Lord's table, you receive your own mystery. You say 'amen' to what you are and by saying it, you subscribe to it."[33] The eucharist, in fact, is the sacramental source of marriage, the memorial sacrifice which the spouses share for their own transformation into the oneness of Christ. Both sacraments actualize the mystery of love which the spouses share in the home and church "liturgies": "This is my body given for you in love."

All rituals of marriage, therefore, should refer to the relationship between eucharist and marriage. The Roman marriage rite usually draws from this relationship moral implications for the life of the spouses. From this relationship derives a theology of the eucharist as a spiritual and personal journey that bonds, empowers, and guides the dynamic yet always unpredictable journey toward the perfection of two imperfect people. The eucharist is, in fact, the festive agape and sacrifice of faith embodying a conscious choice of renewal, thanksgiving, and joy.

## SIGN OF THE NEW COMMUNITY

The sacrament of marriage initiates the family unit in which husband and wife form a new Christian community. In addition to the many factors affecting family life today (for example, cultural and economic factors), this covenantal community includes components that have to be integrated into the whole meaning of human life. These components are relational, social, and ecclesial. Since we have already discussed the first two of these, we will now expand the concept of the family as a sign of a basic Christian community. As a vital ecclesial unit, the family in fact becomes a domestic church, or *ecclesio-*

*la;* as such it can be understood from the theological perspective of the larger family of the church. The family not only relates to the church, but also images the church and has the potential to become a place "where the Gospel is transmitted and from which the Gospel radiates."[34]

### The Paschal Experience: Beginning of the New Community

Like the larger community of the church, the family community of faith proceeds from the same action of Christ and his Spirit. The family becomes a sign of faith when it is imbued with the Spirit, when it is born again of the same community's Spirit. This new theological dimension of marriage is a logical development of today's new ecclesiology. Postconciliar theology reexamined the church's origin and mission from two intimately connected sources upon which the inner nature of Christian marriage also depends: the Christ-event and the Spirit-event—Easter and Pentecost. Church communities came into being through the experience of the risen Lord and under the impact of the Holy Spirit. The risen Lord lives in the church through the action of the Spirit, because "this Lord is the Spirit" (2 Cor 3:17). The church, born and nurtured in the paschal experience is therefore primarily the community and the sacrament of the Spirit.

This biblical perspective is an important contribution to the understanding of marriage that is a sign of a new Christian community. Like the church, marriage as sacrament originating in the glorified body of Christ has in this body the roots of a new existence because the action of the Spirit is the new beginning and power of the risen Christ. As Schussler Fiorenza observes, "A marriage between two individuals is the beginning of a new community of equal disciples and partners under the impact and power of the Spirit."[35]

The church, therefore, is a model for marriage; vice versa, marriage is a model for the church, especially for the local parish and its pastor. Saint John Chrysostom calls the family "a mysterious icon of the church."[36] The domestic church is endowed also with a priestly and prophetic dignity. Both church and family are an organic community of equals which calls for the same spirituality of conversion and committed service.

Both church and family should share the same spirit of fidelity and communion and be characterized by the same virtues of unity, hospitality, and forgiveness. Many of the qualities a priest needs to manifest in his ministry (like mutual respect and sensitivity, accountability and a collaborative attitude, among others) are central to the life of married couples and of families. This idea of partnership in co-responsibility and dialogue is one sign of the birth of a new community, be it church or family.

Marriage cannot be understood by itself, or in a vacuum, and the spouses cannot live their commitment turned in on themselves, or in an exclusively private way. They need to be part of a concrete community and society intimately related to Christ and to the people of God. "A Christian marriage," as Theodore Mackin observes, "is always in the church, of the church and for the church as a community of believers. It is a participation in Christ's work in the world carried on by this community."[37] In the ministerial church, the spouses live in faith their communitarian responsibility. The church continuously renews the couple's baptismal call in the unity of the Spirit through whom they became "a new creature in Christ" (2 Cor 5:17).

### Christ: the Way of the New Community

A Christ-centered spirituality invites the family to witness Christ's love in three primary responsibilities: family relationships, the community of the church, and the secular reality of work and social commitments. These different areas of the social and Christian mission cannot be separated in seeking to follow Christ in all things. As Walter Kasper says, "the laity's secular service also shares in the church's sacramental-symbolic character as the universal sacrament of salvation."[38]

The word of God and liturgical prayer always lead to a Christocentric spirituality. Christ is the center, the source, and the vitality of the family community. Among the many concepts that could be drawn from a biblical and liturgical theology of a new community, the New Testament's central idea of love is an essential key to understanding both the church's and the family's new birth and existence. The community was born out of liberating love of the cross and resurrection of Jesus and becomes his own body: "Now you together are Christ's body" (1 Cor 12:27). The same gift of love builds up the body of the church: "It is love that makes the building grow" (1 Cor 8:1)) and through it the church community becomes Christian witness: "By this love you have for one another, everyone will know that you are my disciples" (Jn 13:35). This is also the reality and goal of the family's spirituality: becoming one body in communion with Christ, becoming builders of his kingdom and witnesses of a new social order based on a community in which equality and justice prevail.

Both the proclaimed word and the liturgical prayer provide a wealth of Christologically inspired themes that apply to community relationships such as love as communion. These themes provide guidelines for married couples and family living. Love is *visible* and calls for human expression (Jn 11:26); it is *open to service*, which is the fundamental sign given to the community (Jn 13:1-6); love is *active* and *real* (1 Jn 3:1-8), *forgiving* (Jn 8:1-8) and *compassionate* (Mt 11:28-29); *it is sacrificial* to accomplish the good of the beloved (Jn 15:13) and at the cost of one's own life (Eph 5:25); love is *unconditional*, an unreserved gift for life (Mk 10:1-22), "as an offering totally free and gratuitous" (Lk 6:27-35);[39] and *life-giving*, because love embodies the very realities of life (1 Jn 3:14-17). As the mystery of an intimate communion, the horizon of love as Paul describes it (1 Cor 13:4-13) will always be the greatest gift realized by the bridegroom and the beloved Jesus.

The current prayers of the nuptial blessing express in traditional terms the transitory nature of marriage together with the sacrament's eschatological character. Thus these prayers call the couple to go beyond the concerns of self-fulfillment by becoming witnesses of the graceful presence and compassion of God; this is their gift of mission through which they serve those in need. This theme is often related to the traditional after-life reward: "Let them be living examples of Christian life . . . witnesses of Christ to others"; "Bear witness to the love of God in this world so that the afflicted and needy will find in you generous friends, and welcome you into the joys of heaven." This liturgical expression of the eschatological dimension needs stronger emphasis. Marriage not only symbolizes the hope of God's *future* kingdom, but also the possible realization of God's *present* kingdom, which is the divine answer to the human longing for true love, justice, and salvation.

### The Spirit: Principle of the New Community

It is essential to emphasize the role of the Holy Spirit in relation to an ecclesiology of communion and to a theology of marriage as both personal and social. The Spirit of Christ is the ultimate origin of every spiritual gift, such as agape-love which is the source of harmony, stability, and hospitality. Agape-love comes from the Spirit and, in the realization of communion with others, returns to God.

In the New Testament, where the affirmation of solidarity and communion are primordial, the Spirit is seen as the principle of the new community's reality, called church or communion because the Spirit is existentially present to it. The Spirit is the guiding presence and the vivifying pledge of the new existence of the community through which God's self-gift is empowered to love. This is also the hope of the domestic church of the family, "and this hope is not deceptive, because the love of God has been poured into our hearts by the Holy Spirit which has been given us" (Rom 5:5). This gift of love and many others characterize the existence of the community led by the Spirit (Gal 5:22-23).

The Holy Spirit has to be seen in relation to the ritualization of marriage and to married life itself because the Spirit is the artisan of sacramental transformation; the Spirit is the power and the sanctity necessary for living out the marital bond of union which is inspired in the hearts of the spouses. Thus a renewal of the liturgies of marriage requires the recovery of a theological content that expresses a spirituality of marriage and family through the language of God's Spirit as the agent of transformation in the integration between worship and life.

In the 1990 rite of marriage the function of the Holy Spirit has been made explicit in five new prayers of the nuptial blessing.[40] This 1990 reform continued the trend of theologically enriching the Roman liturgy by means of an explicit *epiclesis* being the central moment in all sacramental action.

The celebration of marriage is life, the life of the Spirit in the members of the body of the risen Christ who is for us now the "life-giving Spirit" (1 Cor 15:45). In fact, as Augustine says, "The body of Christ cannot live except by the Spirit of Christ."[41] This life is founded and empowered to grow by sacramental participation. From this perspective the celebration of marriage has been called "a liturgical existential epiclesis"[42] whose essential theological content refers to three effects of the Holy Spirit's presence in the spouses: (1) consecration to holiness; (2) transformation through conversion; (3) and empowerment for the building of the kingdom of God within the family and the larger community.

Other modern rituals of marriage have also recaptured the Trinitarian theology of the ancient Christian tradition which emphasized God's grace and presence through the Triune source of empowering of the marriage life. God's ever-present strength, protection, fulfillment and guidance in the lives of the spouses is invoked in this beautiful Presbyterian prayer:

> Eternal God: without your grace no promise is sure. Strengthen ... [the spouses] with the gift of your Spirit, so they may fulfill the vows they have taken. Keep them faithful to each other and to you. Fill them with such a love and joy that they may build a home where no one is a stranger. And guide them by your word to serve you all the days of their lives; through Jesus Christ our Lord, to whom be honor and glory forever and ever. Amen.[43]

The celebration of marriage is life because "the breath of God" (*ruach*) gave life to the first human couple in creation and seals the love of each couple in Christ. His presence transforms the natural event of marriage into a liberating experience in which the partners become co-creators of the community wherein the burdens of one person are the burden of all, and the joy of one person is shared by all.

*Notes*

1. *Gaudium et Spes* 48 (Flannery 950).
2. Ibid. 48 (Flannery 951).

3. "The Synod Propositions," *The Tablet* 235 (1981) 116.

4. "A Message to Christian Families in the Modern World," *Origins* 10 (1980) 323.

5. See Proposition 36 of the bishops from the Synod of    1980; "The Synod Propositions," *The Tablet* 235 (1981) 165.

6. Karl Lehmann, "The Sacramentality of Christian Marriage" in Richard Malone and John C. Connery, ed., *Contemporary Perspectives on Christian Marriage* (Chicago: Loyola University Press, 1984) 94.

7. Edward Schillebeeckx, *Marriage: Human Reality and   Saving Mystery* (New York: Sheed and Ward, 1965) 68-81.

Achille M. Triacca provides a detailed interpretation of the liturgical prayers of the 1969 rite in "La 'Celebrazione' del Matrimonio. Aspetti teologico-liturgici. Contributo alla Spiritualità Sacramentaria e alla Pastorale Liturgica." in *Realtà e valori del sacramento del matrimonio* (Rome: LAS, 1976) esp. 112-119.

8. José Román Flecha, "Abiertos al amor," in *Casarse en el  Señor* (Madrid: PPC, 1985) 110; see Richard J. Clifford,   "Genesis," in Raymond E. Brown and others, eds., *The New Jerome Biblical Commentary* (Englewood Cliffs, N.J.: Prentice Hall, 1990) 11-13.

9. *Lutheran Book of Worship* (Minneapolis: Augsburg   Publishing House, 1978) 203.

10. Francis Schüssler Fiorenza, "Marriage as a Sacrament in Current Systematic Theology," in *Systematic Theology: Roman Catholic Perspectives* (Minneapolis: Fortress Press, 1991) 335-336.

11. For instance, Hos 1-3; Jer 3:31; Ez 16;23; Is 54:62.

12. See Mk 12:19: Heb 13:20; Rv 21:2, 9.

13. Fiorenza, "Marriage as a Sacrament" 332. A complete exegetical study was done by Tibor Horwath who points out two major difficulties: equality is not implied in the biblical notion of covenant (*berith*), and covenant is a changing concept in Scripture; see his "Marriage: Contract? Covenant? Community? Sacrament of Sacraments—Fallible Symbol of Infallible Love,   Revelation of Sin and Love," in *The Sacraments: God's Love and Mercy Actualized*, ed. Francis A. Eigo (The Villanova University Press, 1979) 148-151.

14. Fiorenza, "Marriage as a Sacrament" 330.

15. "Women's original equality with her 'correspondent,' the man, is part of the loss, (after the fall), suggesting that the subordinate place of woman in Israelite society was not intended by God, but is a result of human sin" (Clifford, "Genesis" 12).

16. See Bernard Cook, *Alternative Futures for Worship*, vol. 5, *Christian Marriage* (Collegeville: The Liturgical Press, 1987) 69-73.

17. Rite of Marriage (1969), Nuptial Blessing "B."

18. *Gaudium et Spes* 48 (Flannery 950).

19. Joseph A. Selling, "Twenty Significant Points in the Theology of Marriage and the Family Present in the Teaching of "Gaudium et Spes," *Bijdragen, Tijdschrift voor filosofie en theologie* 43 (1982) 423.

20. Armenian Ritual; A. Raes, *Le Mariage. Sa célébration et sa spiritualité dans les églises d'orient*, Editions de Chevetogne 38 (1959) 88.

21. John Meyerdorff, *Marriage: An Orthodox Perspective* (New York: St. Vladimir's Seminary Press, 1984) 116.

22. See Mk 2:19-20; Mt 9:15; 22: 1-14; 25:1-13; Lk 5:34-35; Jn 3:29; Rv 19:7; 21:2-9; 22:17.

23. P. Grelot, *La Couple humain dans l'Ecriture* (Paris, 1961) 86.

24. G. Boggio, "Temi biblici nel lezionario del matrimonio," *Rivista liturgica* 73 (1976) 535.

25. JoAnn Heany-Hunter, "The RCIA: A Model for Marriage Preparation," *Living Light* 27 (1991) 211; she quotes John Chrysostom, First Baptismal Instruction, in *Baptismal Instructions*, trans. Paul Harkings (Westminster, MD: The Newman Press, 1963) 27.

26. Karl Rahner, "Marriage as Sacrament," *Theological Investigations*, vol. 10 (London: Darton, Longman and Todd, 1973) 220.

27. *Gaudium et Spes* 52 (Flannery 957).

28. Evelyn Eaton and James D. Whitehead, *Marrying Well: Stages on the Journey of Christian Marriage* (New York: Doubleday, 1983) 43.

29. Rite of Marriage (1969), Nuptial Blessing "A."

30. Raes, *Le Mariage* 119-120.

31. *The Mystery of Crowning According to the Maronite Antiochene Church* (Washington, D.C: Diocese of Saint Maron, 1985) 26.

32. Karl Rahner, *The Practice of Faith* (New York: Crossroad, 1983) 178.

33. *Sermo 272* (PL 38:1246).

34. Paul VI, *Evangelii Nuntiandi* 71.

35. Fiorenza, "Marriage as a Sacrament" 330. I approached the topic of the family as domestic church in "Marriage as Worship: A Theological Analogy," *Worship* 62 (1988) 349-353. See Elizabeth and Mulry Tetlow, *Partners in Service* (New York: University Press of America, 1983).

36. *In Epistulam ad Colossenses* (PG 62:387); quoted by P. Evdokimov, *The Sacrament of Love* 139.

37. Theodore Mackin, *Marriage in the Catholic Church: The Marital Sacrament* (New York: Paulist Press, 1989) 676.

38. Walter Kasper, "The Mission of the Laity," *Theology Digest* 35 (1988) 136.

39. Flecha, "Abiertos al amor" 113-117.

40. New Ritual (1990) nos. 74, 140, 172, 242, 244. See "Commentarium" (in French) *Notitiae* 287 (1990) 310-327.

41. *In Johannem* 26: 13, 15 (PL 35:1611).

42. Achille M. Triacca, "Spiritus Sancti Virtutis Infusio: A proposito alcune tematiche theologico-liturgiche testimoniate nell' "Editio Altera" dell' 'Ordo Celebrandi Matrimonium'," *Notitiae* 26 (1990) 365-390.

43. *The Worshipbook* (Philadelphia: Westminster Press, 1970) 67.

# Conclusion

FROM THE PRIMARY CONSIDERATION OF SACRAMENTALITY, THIS study has explored various aspects of marriage: theological, anthropological, historical, ritual, and biblical. Liturgy provided both the basic setting from which the nature of marital sacramentality was approached and, for the most part, the unifying theme of these different areas. Furthermore, this liturgical perspective was extended to other symbolic models which also express the core and the various dimensions of marriage—namely, communion, vocation, and covenant—and thus provided a more comprehensive view of marriage.

The sacramentality of marriage in this broadened sense was also presented within two different historical traditions: the patristic and the medieval. Looking back over the history of Christian marriage was necessary in order to understand the developmental nature of tradition and the new vision of Vatican II which built upon the patristic and medieval traditions. From this background, we attempted to incorporate and expand on the insights developed after Vatican II, as exemplified in the 1990 Roman rite of marriage. From all these perspectives wider parameters of sacramentality emerged as well as a central focus: God's creative and redemptive action in Christ, in which the spouses share. Here we saw the foundation of the sacramentality of marriage and the ultimate meaning of its spiritual, ethical, and relational values.

The experience of worship was, as indicated, the starting point and the fundamental perspective guiding this study. The all-embracing reality of marriage, as permeated by God's presence is, in fact, perfectly expressed through the symbolic actualization of the action of worship. Worship reveals the core, the "mirabile mysterium" which extends to the many-sided reality of marriage. This core is to be found hidden amidst the very ordinary relationship of marriages and families.

This human mystery and saving reality cannot be reduced to its canonical and institutional aspects. These aspects should not be, as they often were in the medieval and Tridentine traditions, at the forefront of the church's theological and pastoral concerns. The need for integrating all the complex dimensions of marriage is a challenging task whose primary objective must be the solicitous care of the couple, not institutional safeguard. The canonical and ecclesial qualifications, the personalist view and social dimension, the secular values and the sacred mystery, the bodily union and the bond of love, the life of the flesh and the life of the Spirit must all be set in a proper perspective and be rooted in the spirituality and practice of the economy of salvation.

The church's ministerial practice should correspond to the high esteem in which marriage is held. To value the experience of married people searching for meaning in their lives makes this possible. This experience is, in fact, an integral part of a genuine theology of marriage.

Consequently this study stressed the two hinges of sacramentality: the interpersonal and graced marital relationship whose essence is love, and the ecclesial dimension through which the qualifications of Christian marriage—namely, faith, baptism, and community—are actualized. Interpreted as they have been through the centuries-long tradition by a church responding to the local cultures and the needs of changing times, all these aspects represent a rich historical mosaic converging into a centerpiece and the only essential constant of Tradition: "Marriage in the Lord" (1 Cor 7:39). This Tradition is a reminder of the holiness of the sacred bond that has its source in and flows from baptismal consecration.

It is this original vision of the baptismal and conjugal way to salvation that remains the essential goal of the future of Christian marriage, as it has been rightly stated:

> The renewal of Christian marriage, then, would seem to be inseparable, finally, from the renewal of baptismal consciousness

and from the profound consequences that will flow therefrom not only for the life of the family, but for the structures of the Church itself. Thus we shall have come full circle, back to the baptismal foundations of "marriage in Christ" with which the Church's theology of marriage began.[1]

Marriage, therefore, was presented in this study as an initiatory sacrament leading to and flowing from the celebration. The sacrament of love is a particular concretization of the baptismal vocation by which the couple searches to be ideally— despite the too common experience of failure—a visible icon of the Bridegroom Jesus. This calls for a realistic and lifelong process of marital growth rooted in baptism and in the eucharist.

No better testimony of these foundations and no better interpretation of Tradition could be presented than the following text of Tertullian quoted in the 1990 rite of marriage:

A marriage embraced, prepared for, celebrated, and lived out daily in the light of faith is the marriage that "the Church arranges, the sacrifice strengthens, upon which the blessing sets a seal, at which angels are present as witness, and to which the Father gives his consent . . . Two are one in hope . . . one in the religion they practice. They are brother and sister, both servants of the same Master; nothing divides them, either in flesh or in spirit. They are, in very truth, two in one flesh; and where there is but one flesh, there is also but one spirit."[2]

## Notes

1. Mark Searle and Kenneth W. Stevenson, *Documents of the Marriage Liturgy* (Collegeville: The Liturgical Press, 1992) 271.
2. *Order of Celebrating Marriage. Second Typical Edition* (Washington, D. C.: International Committee on English in the Liturgy [ICEL], 1992) Draft, introduction, no. 11, p. 9.
Tertullian, *Ad uxorem* 2, VIII, 6 (CCL 1:395); English tr. J. Quasten, *Patrology*, vol. 2 (repr. Christian Classics, Westminster, MD, 1983) 303. Again Tertullian states the mandate to marry a baptized partner. He is not referring to the necessary intervention of clergy in the marriage ceremony, but to the ecclesial implications of Christian marriage; see Tertullien, *A son épouse*, in Sources chrétiennes, vol. 273 (Paris: Les Editions du Cerf, 1980) 191-192 (current studies and commentary).

# Bibliography

## Sources

Deshusses, J. *Le Sacramentaire Grégorien*, vol. 1, Spicilegium Friburgense, vol. 16. Fribourg: University Press, 1991.

John Paul II, Pope. *Familiaris Consortio: The Apostolic Exhortation on
the Family*. Origins 11:28/29 (December 1981). Also published by
New World Publishing Company, Chicago, 1982.

*Lutheran Book of Worship*. Minneapolis: Augsburg Publishing House,
1978.

*Marriage: Ritual and Pastoral Notes*. Ottawa: Canadian Conference of
Catholic Bishops, 1979.

Mohlberg, L. K., P. Siffrin, and L. Eizenhofer. *Liber Sacramentorum
Romanae Ecclesiae*, REDMF 4. Rome: Herder, 1960. No. 1443-1455.

Mohlberg, L.K., L. Eizenhofer, and P. Siffrin. *Sacramentarium Veronense*, REDMF 1. Rome: Herder, 1955-1956. No. 1105-1110.

National Conference of Catholic Bishops. *An Assessment of the Plan of
Pastoral Action for Family Ministry and the Decade of the Family*.
Washington, D.C.: United States Catholic Conference, 1990).

National Conference of Catholic Bishops. *Faithful to Each Other Forever: A Catholic Handbook of Pastoral Help for Marriage Preparation*.
Washington, D.C.: United States Catholic Conference, 1989.

National Conference of Catholic Bishops. *Putting Children and Families First: A Challenge for Church, Nation, and World*. Origins 21:25
(November 28, 1991).

*Ordo Celebrandi Matrimonium*. Vatican City: Typis Polyglottis, 1969.

*Ordo Celebrandi Matrimonium.* Editio Typica Altera. Vatican City: Typis Polyglottis, 1990.

*Order of Celebrating Marriage. Second Typical Edition.* Washington, D.C.: International Committee on English in the Liturgy (ICEL), 1992 (Draft).

Raes, A. *Le Mariage dans les églises d'Orient.* Chevetogne: Editions, 1958.

*Rituale Romanum.* Ratisbon: Pustet, 1925.

Saint Augustine. *Treatise on Marriage and Other Subjects.* Edited by Roy J. Deferrari. Washington: The Catholic University of America, 1955.

Searle, Mark and Kenneth W. Stevenson, eds. *Documents of the Marriage Liturgy.* Collegeville: The Liturgical Press, 1992.

*The Worshipbook.* Philadelphia: Westminster Press, 1970.

*The Book of Common Prayer.* New York: The Church Hymnal Corporation and the Seabury Press, 1977.

*The Book of Services.* Nashville: The United Publishing House, 1984.

### Literature

Anzia, Joan Meyer, and Mary G. Durkin. *Marital Intimacy: A Catholic Perspective.* Kansas City: Andrews and McMeel, 1980.

Babos, Stephen. "Marriage as a Sacrament." *Thought* 58 (1983) 5-17.

Barth, Karl. *The Doctrine of Creation.* Vol. 3, pt. 4 of *Church Dogmatics.* Edinburgh: T and T Clark, 1961) 116-323.

Bellah, Robert N. "The Church as the Context for the Family." *New Oxford Review* (December 1987) 6-13.

Brundage, James A. *Law, Sex, and Christian Society in Medieval Europe.* Chicago: University of Chicago Press, 1987.

Buber, Martin. *I and Thou.* New York: Charles Scribner's Sons, 1970.

Cahill, Lisa. *Between the Sexes: Foundations for a Christian Ethics of Sexuality.* Philadelphia: Fortress Press, 1985.

Carmody, Denise Lardner. *Caring for Marriage.* New York: Paulist Press, 1985.

Champlin, Joseph. *The Marginal Catholic: Challenge, Don't Crush.* Notre Dame: Ave Maria Press, 1989.

Chupungco, Anscar. "The Cultural Adaptation of the Rite of Marriage." In *La Celebrazione Cristiana Del Matrimonio,* ed. G. Farnedi, Studia Anselmiana, vol. 93. Rome: Pontificio Ateneo S. Anselmo, 1986. 145-162.

Cooke, Bernard. ed. *Christian Marriage: Alternative Futures for Worship,* vol. 5. Collegeville: The Liturgical Press, 1987.

Covino, Paul. ed. *Celebrating Marriage: Preparing the Wedding Liturgy.* Washington, D.C.: The Pastoral Press, 1988.

Curran, Dolores. *Traits of a Healthy Family.* San Francisco: Harper and Row, 1983.

Davis, Charles. *Body as Spirit.* New York: Seabury Press, 1976.

Del Vecchio, Anthony and Mary Del Vecchio. *Preparing for the Sacrament of Marriage.* Notre Dame: Ave Maria Press, 1980.

Denneny, Raymond, ed. *Christian Married Love.* San Francisco: Ignatius Press, 1981.

Denton, Wallace, ed. *Marriage and Family Enrichment.* New York: Haworth Press, 1986.

DeYonker, John F. and Thomas E. Tobin. *Your Marriage.* Liguori, MO: Liguori Publications, 1976.

Dominian, Jack. *Marriage, Faith and Love.* New York: Crossroad, 1982.

Doyle, Thomas P. *Marriage Studies: Reflections in Canon Law and Theology,* vol. 3. Washington, D.C.: Catholic University of   America: Canon Law Society of America, 1984.

Durkin, Mary G. *Making Your Family Work.* Chicago: Thomas More, 1988.

Evenou, J. "Marriage." In *The Church at Prayer,* vol. 3, *The Sacraments.* Collegeville: The Liturgical Press, 1988) 185-207.

Everett, William Johnson. *Blessed Be the Bond: Christian Perspectives on Marriage and Family.* Lanham, MD: University Press of America, 1990.

Fiorenza, Francis Schüssler. "Marriage." In F. Schüssler Fiorenza and John P. Galvin, eds., *Systematic Theology: Roman Catholic Perspectives.* Minneapolis: Fortress Press, 1991. 307-346.

Fisher, Kathleen and Thomas Hart. *Promises to Keep—Developing the Skills of Marriage.* New York: Paulist Press, 1991.

Francis, Mark R. *Liturgy in a Multicultural Community.* Collegeville: The Liturgical Press, 1991.

Freidman, Edwin H. *Generation to Generation.* New York: Guilford Press, 1985.

Gallagher, Charles A. and others. *Embodied in Love: Sacramental Spirituality and Sexual Intimacy.* New York: Crossroad, 1984.

Haring, Bernhard. *No Way Out? Pastoral Care of the Divorced and Remarried.* Midlegreen, Slough, England: St. Paul Publications, 1990.

_____. *Marriage in the Modern World.* Westminster, MD: Newman Press, 1965.

Hart, Thomas. *Living Happily Everafter: Toward a Theology of Christian Marriage.* New York: Paulist Press, 1979.

Haughton, Rosemary. *The Passionate God.* New York: Paulist Press, 1981.

Hiesberger, Jean M., ed. *Preparing for Marriage Handbook*. New York: Paulist Press, 1980.

Hunter, David G., ed. *Marriage in the Early Church*. Minneapolis: Fortress Press, 1992.

Imbiorski, Walter J. and John L. Thomas. *Beginning Your Marriage*. Chicago: Delaney, 1971.

Kasper, Walter. *Theology of Christian Marriage*. New York: Crossroad, 1983.

Kerns, Joseph. *The Theology of Marriage*. New York: Sheed and Ward, 1964.

Kosnik, Anthony, and others. *Human Sexuality: New Directions in American Catholic Thought*. New York: Paulist, 1977.

Lawler, Michael G. *Secular Marriage, Christian Sacrament*. Mystic, CT: Twenty-Third Publications, 1985.

_____. *Ecumenical Marriage and Remarriage: Gifts and Challenges to the Churches*. Mystic, CT: Twenty-Third Publications, 1990.

_____. "Sacrament of Marriage." In *The Dictionary of Sacramental Worship*. Edited by Peter E. Fink. Collegeville, MN: The Liturgical Press, 1990. 805-818.

L'Abate, Luciane. *Building Family Competence*. Newbury Park, CA: Sage Publ., 1990.

LeMaire, H. Paul. *Marrying Takes a Lifetime*. Mystic, CT: Twenty-Third Publications, 1981.

Luther, Martin. *The Estate of Marriage*. In *Luther's Works*, vol. 45. Edited by Walter Brandt. Philadelphia: Muhlenberg Press, 1962.

Mackin, Theodore. *The Marital Sacrament*. New York: Paulist Press, 1989.

_____. *Divorce and Remarriage*. New York: Paulist Press, 1984.

_____. *Marriage in the Catholic Church: What is Marriage?* New York: Paulist Press, 1982.

Malone, Richard and John R. Connery, eds. *Contemporary Perspectives on Christian Marriage*. Chicago: Loyola University Press, 1984.

Martin Thomas M. *The Challenge of Christian Marriage: Marriage in Scripture, History and Contemporary Life*. New York: Paulist Press, 1990.

Meyendorff, John. *Marriage: An Orthodox Perspective*. New York: St. Vladimir's Seminary Press, 1970.

Nelson, James. *Embodiment: An Approach to Sexuality and Christian Theology*. Minneapolis: Augsburg, 1978.

Orsy, Ladislas. *Marriage in Canon Law*. Wilmington, DE: Michael Glazier, 1986.

Palmer, Paul. "Christian Marriage: Contract or Covenant?" *Theological Studies* 33 (1972) 617-665.

Phillips, Roderick. *Putting Asunder: A History of Divorce in Western Society*. New York: Cambridge University Press, 1988.

Preister, Steve. *Families, Church and Society*. Washington, D.C.: Catholic Charities Social Thought, vol. 2, 1990.

Rahner, Karl. "Marriage as Sacrament." In *Theological Investigations*, vol. 10. New York: Seabury Press, 1974.

Roberts, William P., ed. *Commitment to Partnership: Explorations of the Theology of Marriage*. New York: Paulist Press, 1987.

Ruether, Rosemary, ed. *Religion and Sexism*. New York: Simon and Schuster, 1974.

Scheeben, Matthias Joseph. *The Mysteries of Christianity*. St. Louis: B. Herder, 1946.

Sawyers, Lindell, ed. *Faith and Families*. Philadelphia: The Geneva Press, 1986.

Schillebeeckx, Edward. *Marriage: Secular Reality and Saving Mystery*. New York: Sheed and Ward, 1965.

Schmeiser, J.M. "Marriage: New Developments in the Diocese of Autun, France." *Eglise et Théologie* 10 (1979) 369-386.

Scott, Kieran and Michael Warren, eds. *Perspectives on Marriage: A Reader*. New York: Oxford University Press, 1993.

Sloyan, G.S. "The New Rite for Celebrating Marriage." *Worship* 44 (1970) 258-267.

Stevenson, Kenneth. *Nuptial Blessing: A Study of Christian Marriage Rites*. New York: Oxford University Press, 1982.

Stone, Lawrence. *The Past and the Present*. Boston: Routledge and Kegan Paul, 1981.

Thomas, David M. *Christian Marriage: A Journey Together*. Wilmington, DE: Michael Glazier, 1983.

_____. "Marriage." In *Dictionary of Catholic Spirituality*. Collegeville: The Liturgical Press, 1993.

Turner, Victor. *The Ritual Process*. London: Routledge and Kegan Paul, 1969.

Van Gennep, Arnold. *Les Rites de passage*. Paris: Librairie Critique, Emile Mourry, 1909.

Whitehead, James, and Evelyn Whitehead. *Marrying Well: Stages on the Journey of Christian Marriage*. New York: Doubleday, 1984.

_____. *A Sense of Sexuality: Christian Love and Intimacy*. New York: Doubleday, 1989.

Wood, Susan. "The Marriage of Baptized Nonbelievers: Faith, Contract, and Sacrament." *Theological Studies* 48 (1987) 279-301.

Yates, Wilson. "The Protestant View of Marriage." *Journal of Ecumenical Studies* 22 (1985) 41-54.